Building Character Schoolwide

Creating a Caring Community in Your School

Principal/Teacher's Guide

Rudy Bernardo
Linda Frye
Deborah Smith
Genieve Foy

ISBN 1-892056-10-0
$18.00

Cover design by Paul Turley
Book design by Sara Sanders

Contents

Acknowledgments

This book is a product of love. It is particularly appropriate to note that innumerable souls played a part in the creation of this book. Special credit, however is publicly acknowledged to the following:

To the students of Allen Classical/Traditional Academy and Broadmoor Academy, for whom the challenge to develop and strengthen the character education program emerged; the teachers, staff, and parents of Allen and Broadmoor who responded to the challenge and thus created a positive culture and climate in the school.

To our spouses and children whose love, understanding, and support sustained and increased our inspiration.

Preface

This guide is dedicated to all teachers, administrators, and all other school staff, working directly or indirectly with school children. It is our hope that the ideas, stories, quotations cited in this guide will help you, help children on how to understand, avoid, and solve problems; learn to accept discipline with courage rather than with resentment.

Punctuality

DEFINITION:
Acting finished or arriving on time; to be punctual with work.

MONDAY: The trait of the week is punctuality. To be punctual means to be on time. Our world runs on time and we must be punctual or we will miss things. Today, discuss what our lives will be like if buses, schools, businesses, and other establishments will not operate on time. What are the benefits of being punctual?

TUESDAY: The trait of the week is punctuality. To be punctual means to be on time. It is important for each of us to come to school on time and leave on time. You are to be here when school starts at 8:40 a.m. 8:00 is too early and 10:00 is too late. Today, discuss how someone coming to class late or leaving early upsets the school day.

WEDNESDAY: The trait of the week is punctuality. To be punctual means to be on time. Your mother told you that she would pick you up after school at 2:30 p.m. She was late. She arrived at 3:30. How you will feel if someone has told you that he/she will pick you up at a certain time and he/she was late or never showed up?

THURSDAY: The trait of the week is punctuality. To be punctual means to be on time. As children you depend a great deal on parents and other adults to help you to be punctual. You, however, have the opportunity to learn to be punctual yourself. When the recess whistle blows, are you punctual lining up? When you leave your classroom for lunch do you dawdle and fuss around or are you lined up and ready to go? Today, discuss how each of you can practice being punctual.

FRIDAY: The trait of the week is punctuality. To be punctual means to be on time. Today is Friday. We've spent a week discussing how to be punctual and how it feels if someone is not punctual. We've talked about how, as children, you can practice being punctual. Sometimes we cannot help being late for an appointment. Today, discuss things you can do if you know you cannot be punctual.

Thoughts to Ponder:

"Dost thou love life? Then do not squander time; for that's the stuff life is made of."

Benjamin Franklin

"Punctuality is the politeness of kings."

Louis XV!

"An inch of gold will not buy and inch of time."

Chinese proverb

"I owe all my success in life to having been always a quarter of a hour before hand."

Lord Nelson

"The early bird gets the worm."

Old proverb

Suggested Books:

In for Winter, Out for Spring, Arnold Adoff

Mary Alice, Operator Number 9, Jeffery Allen

The Berenstain Bears and Too much Pressure, Stan and Jan Berenstain

Joe on Sunday, Tony Blundell

I Met a Polar Bear, Selma and Pauline Boyd

Time to Get Out of the Bath, Shirley, John Burningham

The Grouchy Ladybug, Eric Carle

Today is Monday, Eric Carle

It's About Time Jesse Bear, Nancy White Carlstrom

What if the Bus Doesn't Come?, Gineet Lamont Clarke and Florence Stevens

Time for Bed, Mem Fox

Waiting for Jennifer, Kathryn Osebold Galbraith

The Sun's Day, Mordicai Gerstein

Clocks and More Clocks, Pat Hutchins

Is It Time?, Marilyn Janovitz

Big Time Bears, Stephen Krensky

Time to..., Bruce McMillan

Around the Clock with Harriet, Betsy and Guilio Maestro

Waiting for Noah, Shulamith Levey Oppenheim

Bakery Business, W.B. Park

Henry's Important Date, Robert Quackenbush

Bear Child's Book of Hours, Anne Rockwell

Nine O'Clock Lullaby, Marilyn Singer

Clocks in the Woods, Leon Steinmetz

Waiting, Nicki Weiss

(For a complete annotated listing of these books see the bibliography, page 77.)

Promptness

DEFINITION:
Ready, quick; on time, punctual

MONDAY: The trait of the week is promptness. Promptness means to be on time. Students are asked to be prompt with homework and arrival to school. What does that mean? If you arrive at school on time you are prompt. That means you are here and ready to begin the day's work with your classmates. It is important to be here on time so that you don't miss activities in your classroom. Discuss things you can do to be prompt.

TUESDAY: The trait of the week is promptness. Promptness means to be on time. Yesterday we talked about things you can do to be prompt. Today lets talk about Billy. Before going to bed, Billy puts all his school supplies, books, and homework in his book bag. He sets his alarm clock. Discuss what Billy did to be prompt or on time for school the next day.

WEDNESDAY: The trait of the week is promptness. Promptness means to be on time. When you practice this week's trait, promptness, people can see you know how to manage your time. It shows that you are a responsible person. You are reliable and dependable. Today, discuss some of the traits of Abraham Lincoln that made him a great person.

THURSDAY: The trait of the week is promptness. Promptness means to be on time. In your class, discuss the consequences of doctors, police, fire or ambulance workers not being prompt. Why is it necessary? What might happen if these workers would not be concerned about being prompt to act?

FRIDAY: The trait of the week is promptness. Promptness means to be on time. We have talked all week about the word prompt. Are you being more careful about getting to school on time and turning in homework? Discuss some ways that you have tried that are being successful and helping you with promptness. Perhaps some of your suggestions will be of help to others.

Thoughts to Ponder:

"I recommend you take care of the minutes for the hours will take care of themselves."

Lord Chesterfield (Letter to His Son)

"An inch of gold will not buy an inch of time."

Chinese proverb

"The time is always right to do what is right."

Martin Luther King Jr.

"The past, the present, and the future are really one—they are today."

Stowe

"We live in the present, we dream of the future, and we learn eternal truths from the past."

Madame Chiang Kai-shek

Suggested Books:

In for Winter, Out for Spring, Arnold Adoff

Mary Alice, Operator Number 9, Jeffery Allen

The Berenstain Bears and Too much Pressure, Stan and Jan Berenstain

Joe on Sunday, Tony Blundell

I Met a Polar Bear, Selma and Pauline Boyd

Time to Get Out of the Bath, Shirley, John Burningham

The Grouchy Ladybug, Eric Carle

Today is Monday, Eric Carle

It's About Time Jesse Bear, Nancy White Carlstrom

What if the Bus Doesn't Come?, Gineet Lamont Clarke and Florence Stevens

Time for Bed, Mem Fox

Waiting for Jennifer, Kathryn Osebold Galbraith

The Sun's Day, Mordicai Gerstein

Clocks and More Clocks, Pat Hutchins

Is It Time?, Marilyn Janovitz

Big Time Bears, Stephen Krensky

Time to..., Bruce McMillan

Around the Clock with Harriet, Betsy and Guilio Maestro

Waiting for Noah, Shulamith Levey Oppenheim

Bakery Business, W.B. Park

Henry's Important Date, Robert Quackenbush

Bear Child's Book of Hours, Anne Rockwell

Nine O'Clock Lullaby, Marilyn Singer

Clocks in the Woods, Leon Steinmetz

Waiting, Nicki Weiss

(For a complete annotated listing of these books see the bibliography, page 77.)

Readiness

DEFINITION: Prepared for immediate use of action. To be mentally and physically prepared for an experience or an action.

MONDAY: The trait of the week is readiness. To be ready means to be prepared for immediate use of action. Each day you should come to school ready to learn. If you are prepared for school, you will have all the tools and books you need for class. Today with your teacher discuss how you can come to class prepared to learn.

TUESDAY: The trait of the week is readiness. To be ready means to be prepared for immediate use of action. Yesterday you discussed ways that you could be prepared for class each day. Some of your answers may have included having paper, pencils. Completed homework, and textbooks. You can also do things at home to help prepare you for school. One thing that you could do is to get enough sleep each night. Discuss with your teacher things that you can do at home to help you be ready for school each day.

WEDNESDAY: The trait of the week is readiness. To be ready means to be prepared for immediate use of action. Yesterday you discussed what you could do at home that would help you to be ready for school. Today discuss manners, behavior in the lunchroom. How to prepare yourself for a good lunch.

THURSDAY: The trait of the week is readiness. To be ready means to be prepared for immediate use of action. Today talk about successful people in your school/community. Discuss what they did to be successful in life. List all the traits that made them successful.

FRIDAY: The trait of the week is readiness. To be ready means to be prepared for immediate use of action. Yesterday you talk about successful people in your school/community, what they did to be successful. Today talk about what you are doing in your school to prepare yourself for the next grade.

Thoughts to Ponder:

"The great secret of success in life is to be ready when opportunity comes."

Benjamin Disraeli

"The best preparation for tomorrow's work is to do your work as well as you can today."

Elbert Hubbard

"Be prepared."

Scout Motto

"Most people put off until tomorrow that which they should have done yesterday."

Edgar W. Howe

"Yesterday is a cancelled check; tomorrow is a promissory note; today is ready cash—spend it...wisely."

Author unknown

Suggested Books

A Weed Is a Flower: The Life of George Washington Carver, Aliki

First Grade Can Wait, Lorraine Aseltine

I Want to Be an Astronaut, Thomas Y. Crowell

Everyone Ready?, Franz Brandenberg

Timothy Turtle, Al Graham

Little Toot, Hardie Gramatky

Henry's Wild Morning, Margaret Greaves

Ben's Trumpet, Rachel Isadora

When I See My Dentist..., Susan Kuklin

When I See My Doctor..., Susan Kuklin

The Solo, Kathryn Lasky

Johnny's Eggs, Earlene Long

Andrew's Bath, David McPhail

Where's Jenna?, Margaret Miller

Dance, Tanya, Satomi Ichikawa

Tacky the Penguin, Helen Lester

Pig Pig Gets a Job, David McPhail

Ready, Alice?, Margo Mason

Be Ready at Eight, Peggy Parish

Alistair's Time Machine, Marilyn Sadler

Nobody Has Time for Me, Vladimir Skutina

Is Susan Here?, Janice May Udry

Harry Gets Ready for School, Harriet Ziefert

(For a complete annotated listing of these books see the bibliography, page 96.)

Responsibility

DEFINITION: The condition of being responsible; Obliged to carry out or take care of, as duty, trust or debt; Reliable, trustworthy.

MONDAY: The trait of the week is responsibility. To be responsible means to be able to carry out a duty and to be trustworthy. As we grow older, we are expected to accept more responsibility for our actions. Today, discuss and make a list of responsibilities that you have in your home/school.

TUESDAY: The trait of the week is responsibility. To be responsible means to be able to carry out a duty and to be trustworthy. Today, talk about responsibilities and how it affects people around us. Think of this old poem: For want of a nail a shoe was lost/ for want of a shoe a horse was lost/ for want of a horse the battle was lost/ for want of a battle the war was lost…all for the want of a single nail. You can help everybody you meet today by being a responsible person. Don't you be the one to lose the nail!

WEDNESDAY: The trait of the week is responsibility. To be responsible means to be able to carry out a duty and to be trustworthy. Responsibility is very important part of what we do. Only when we become responsible can we hope to become independent. Let's talk about an area of responsibility—lunch money. Every day each of you know you will be going through the lunch line. You know you will need lunch money. Every day we have students come to the office and say, "My mom forgot to give me my lunch money." What's wrong with this picture? MY MOM? But guess what! It's not mom's job to remember your lunch money. It's your job. If you have lunch money problem, its because you forgot to ask your lunch money. That's called responsibility—carrying our one's duty.

THURSDAY: The trait of the week is responsibility. To be responsible means to be able to carry out a duty and to be trustworthy. As we grow older we are expected to assume more responsibility. Today, talk about successful people. What made them successful? Why are they responsible people?

FRIDAY: The trait of the week is responsibility. To be responsible means to be able to carry out a duty and to be trustworthy. We all have responsibilities, both at home and at our job. Students—your job is school. Discuss and make a list of responsibilities that you have in school.

Thoughts to Ponder:

" You cannot escape the responsibility of tomorrow by evading it today."

Abraham Lincoln

"If each one sweeps before his own door, the whole street will be clean."

Yiddish proverb

"You cannot do more than your duty; you should never wish to do less."

Robert E. Lee

"Do your job with your whole heart and you will succeed—there is so little competition."

Elbert Hubbard

"There is not a moment without some duty."

Cicero

Suggested Books:

Miss Nelson Has a Field Day, Henry Allard

Shoeshine Girl, Robert Clyde Bulla

Mike Mulligan and His Steam Shovel, Virginia Lee Burton

The Little Red Hen, Paul Galdone

Responsibility: What Is It?, N. Pemberton and J. Riehecky

Horton Hears a Who!, Dr. Seuss

Taking Care of Melvin, Marjorie Weinman Sharmat

The Little Engine That Saved the City, Dennis Smith

A Bird's Best Friend, Tish Sommers

The Gift of the Tree, Alvin Tresselt

I Think He likes Me, Elizabeth Winthrop

(For a complete annotated listing of these books see the bibliography, page 82.)

Respectfulness

DEFINITION: To have or show high regard for; the state of being esteemed; to treat with courtesy or consideration.

MONDAY: The trait of the week is respectfulness. To be respectful means to honor them, esteem them, and hold them in high regard. We talk a lot at school about showing respect for adults or those who have positions of authority over you. Today, talk about ways to demonstrate respect for adults and authority figures.

TUESDAY: The trait of the week is respectfulness. To be respectful means to honor them, esteem them, and hold them in high regard. We show our respect to others by treating them the way we wish to be treated. Today practice being respectful by using your very best manners.

WEDNESDAY: The trait of the week is respectfulness. To be respectful means to honor them, esteem them, and hold them in high regard. We have been taught to respect the authority. Authorities deserve our respect because of the responsibilities they have pledged to fulfill. Today, express your appreciation to at least one of your authority figures, a parent, your teachers, the principal, or another that helps you through your day.

THURSDAY: The trait of the week is respectfulness. To be respectful means to honor them, esteem them, and hold them in high regard. How do we show respect for our peers? Well, we listen to them without interrupting when they are talking to us. We do not say unkind or untrue things about them. We use appropriate voice volume and tone—we do not call names. Today, at recess, demonstrate respect for your peers.

FRIDAY: The trait of the week is respectfulness. To be respectful means to honor them, esteem them, and hold them in high regard. Today we are going to discuss respect for you. You know this is the easiest one because every time you treat someone else with respect, you are respecting yourself. When you follow rules, speak appropriately and kindly to others, fulfill your responsibilities, do your best—you are being respectful. Along with this is taking care of you. Keeping yourself clean, your clothing clean is being respectful. Respect yourself and respect others—this one quality alone can help open many doors for you as you go through life.

Thoughts to Ponder:

"The value of man should be seen in what he gives and not in what he is able to receive."

Albert Einstein

"Every action done in company, ought to be with some sign of respect to those that are present."

George Washington

"We must learn to live together as bothers or perish together as fools."

Martin Luther King Jr.

"A bit of fragrance always clings to the hand that gives you roses."

Chinese proverb

"I keep my ideals, because in spite of everything, I still believe that people are really good at heart."

Anne Frank

Suggested Books:

Fish and Flamingo, Nancy White Carlstrom

Great Kapok Tree, Lynne Cherry

Watch Out for Chicken Feet in Your Soup, Tomie De Paola

Are You My Friend?, Janice Derby

Respect, Beverly Fiday and Deborah Crowdy

Good Morning, Good Night, Ivan Gantschev

Just About Perfect, Kate Green

The Lady and the Spider, Faith NcNutly

Cocoon, Diane Redfield Massie

The Porcupine Mouse, Bonnie Pryor

Python's Party, Brian Wildsmith

(For a complete annotated listing of these books see the bibliography, page 83.)

Dependability

> **DEFINITION:** The quality of being dependable, reliability; worthy of trust.

MONDAY: The trait of the week is dependability. Dependability means capable of being relied upon. Each of us has dependable people in our lives. They are the people we trust to do what needs to be done. At school we depend on our custodians to keep our school and playground safe and clean. We have dependable people fixing our lunch each day. We depend on our teachers to help us learn. Today list jobs at school and how we depend on these people to do what must be done.

TUESDAY: The trait of the week is dependability. Dependability means capable of being relied upon. Yesterday, we talked about dependable people here at school. They can be trusted to do what they say they are going to do. We also have dependable people at home. No matter who we live with, we count on adults in our life to do things for us because they must be done. Today, please discuss and list the everyday things at home we trust other people to do for us.

WEDNESDAY: The trait of the week is dependability. Dependability means capable of being relied upon. We have discussed how we trust and rely on dependable people in our lives. Those people became dependable by being given tasks to do and then doing them. As student at (name of school) you also have jobs and responsibilities which help you develop dependability. We trust you to come to school on time, we depend on you to have all pencils and papers you need. Today, list some ways your teacher and other adults depend on you.

THURSDAY: The trait of the week is dependability. Dependability means capable of being relied upon. Billy is on traffic patrol. Mr. Lekan, the school custodian has also asked him, to help put up the flag each day. Billy takes this responsibility seriously. One day Billy was ill and could not go to school. He called Steve, another patrol member, and asked him to help Mr. Lekan put up the flag. When Billy was unable to do the job, he wanted to make sure it was still done. Is Billy a dependable person? Why?

FRIDAY: The trait of the week is dependability. Dependability means capable of being relied upon. We have been discussing being dependable. Other words we've used with dependable are trust, count on, and rely on. What happens when we can't depend on others to do what we trust them to do? Today, discuss what would happen if we didn't have dependable people around us.

Thoughts to Ponder:

"There are two very difficult things in the world. One is to make a name for oneself and the other is to keep it."

Robert Schumann

"You cannot escape the responsibility of tomorrow by evading it today."

Abraham Lincoln

"To be trusted is a greater compliment than to be loved."

George MacDonald

"A promise made is a debt unpaid."

Robert William Service

Suggested Books:

Miss Nelson Has a Field Day, Henry Allard

Shoeshine Girl, Robert Clyde Bulla

Mike Mulligan and His Steam Shovel, Virginia Lee Burton

The Little Red Hen, Paul Galdone

Responsibility: What Is It?, N. Pemberton and J. Riehecky

Horton Hears a Who!, Dr. Seuss

Taking Care of Melvin, Marjorie Weinman Sharmat

The Little Engine That Saved the City, Dennis Smith

A Bird's Best Friend, Tish Sommers

The Gift of the Tree, Alvin Tresselt

I Think He likes Me, Elizabeth Winthrop

(For a complete annotated listing of these books see the bibliography, page 82.)

Obedience

DEFINITION: The act, habit, or condition of obeying; compliance, as with rules, regulations, or laws.

MONDAY: The trait of the week is obedience. To be obedient means to follow rules, regulations, or laws. Are you obedient? Are more people obedient? What would the world be like if people willingly followed laws, rules, regulations? In your class, discuss what you think a PERFECT world would be like.

TUESDAY: The trait of the week is obedience. To be obedient means to follow rules, regulations, or laws. Yesterday, you discussed about what you think a perfect world would be like. Today, use your imagination and for a little while, try to imagine a world with NO laws. What would be the immediate consequences?

WEDNESDAY: The trait of the week is obedience. To be obedient means to follow rules, regulations, or laws. Let me tell you a story of Billy and his father. When Billy was five, he and his father went for a drive in the country. At the crossroads, Billy's father drove through the red light, without bothering to stop. Billy said. "Daddy, in school my teacher taught us that we are supposed to stop at every stop light" His father replied, "oh, don't worry son. There's no traffic on this road, and besides, there are no police cars around. No one will ever see us going through the red light." In you class discuss what Billy's father did that are wrong?

THURSDAY: The trait of the week is obedience. To be obedient means to follow rules, regulations, or laws. Today, let me read to you a quote from our 30th President, Calvin Coolidge. He said, "I sometimes wish people would put a little more emphasis upon following the law than they do upon its enforcement. Discuss with your class the meaning of this statement.

FRIDAY: The trait of the week is obedience. To be obedient means to follow rules, regulations, or laws. Yesterday, we discussed a quote from President Calvin Coolidge. He said, "I sometimes wish people would put a little more emphasis upon following the law than they do upon its enforcement." Today, draw a picture showing someone obeying a rule or law. Take it home. Show it to your family. Tell them what you have learned about obedience.

Thoughts to Ponder:

"No man is above the law and no man is below it; nor do we ask any man's permission when we require him to obey it."

Theodore Roosevelt

"Character lies in obedience to the law, irrespective of whether one likes the law, believes in it, or is opposed to it."

John D. Rockefeller Jr.

"The very idea of the power and right of the people to establish government presupposes the duty of every individual to obey the established government."

George Washington

Suggested Books:

Who Keeps Us Safe?, Caroline Arnold

Wagon Wheels, Barbara Brenner

Safe Sally Seatbelt and the Magic Click, Phyliss Gobbell and Jim Laster

The Ox-Cart Man, Donald Hall

What If Everybody Did That?, Ellen Javernick

John Henry: An American Legend, Ezra Jack Keats

The Foxbury Force, Graham Oakley

Granny and the Desperadoes, Peggy Parish

Pleasant Pig and the Terrible Dragon, Richard Scarry

The Great Mystery Book, Richard Scarry

(For a complete annotated listing of these books see the bibliography, page 85.)

Self-Control

DEFINITION:
Control of one's emotions or actions.

MONDAY: The trait of the week is self-control. Self-control means control of one's emotions or actions. All of us know—deep down, that we ourselves have the sole power to control ourselves. Who decides or controls where your hands and feet go? Who decides or controls what comes out of our mouth? You do, of course? Discuss today how to develop self-control.

TUESDAY: The trait of the week is self-control. Self-control means control of one's emotions or actions. Yesterday we discussed self-control and ways of helping ourselves make good decisions. I noticed some of you thought of counting to 10 before acting and of asking yourself, "is this actions or are these words going to help this situation or make this situation worse? These are good strategies in learning self-control. Self-control is also helpful in doing homework. Discuss today how self-control is important in fulfilling homework responsibilities.

WEDNESDAY: The trait of the week is self-control. Self-control means control of one's emotions or actions. When you have homework responsibilities you need to exercise self-control in choosing the time to do it, in getting rid of distractors (like tv, stereo, radio) and in managing your time so that you allow enough time to get it completed. Share with your classmates how you manage your time and develop self-control.

THURSDAY: The trait of the week is self-control. Self-control means control of one's emotions or actions. We have talked about self-control and how it can help us with discipline and with homework. Today, let us talk about self-control in the lunchroom. By controlling our actions and emotions we will: 1) remember to pick up our milk and silverware and all the items we need for lunch. 2) keep our voices calm and reasonable. 3) keep our hands and feet to ourself. Each of us has control over one person and that is ourselves.

FRIDAY: The trait of the week is self-control. Self-control means control of one's emotions or actions. Our discussion of self-control this week has shown us the benefits of exercising restraint over our behavior. Self-control is very powerful. With self-control, we are strong individuals. Without self-control, we give up power and are victims. Make good positive choices to remain strong individuals.

Thoughts to Ponder:

"If it is not right, do not do it; if it is not true, do not say it."

Marcus Aurelius

"If I have the belief that I can do it, I shall surely acquire the capacity to do it even if I may not have it at the beginning."

Mahatma Gandhi

"Even if you're on the right track you'll get run over if you just sit there."

Will Rogers

"We judge ourselves by what we feel capable of doing. But other judge us by what we have already done."

Henry W. Longfellow

Suggested Books:

Donald Says Thumbs Down, Nancy Evans Cooney

The Strongest One of All, Mirra Ginsburg

Help, Laura Greene

Sara and the Door, Virginia Allen Jensen

I Can Do It By Myself, Lessie Jones Little and Eloise Greenfield

I Was So Mad, Mayer Mercer

The Little Engine That Could, Piper Watty

Can I Help?, Anne and Harlow Rockwell

Oliver, Amanda and Grandmother Pig, Jean Val Leeuwen

I Can Ride It!, Shigeo Watanabe

Where's My Daddy?, Shigeo Watanabe

I Can Build a House, Shigeo Watanabe

Someday, Sied Mitchell, Barbara Williams

The Hating Book, Charlotte Zolotow

(For a complete annotated listing of these books see the bibliography, page 80.)

Politeness

DEFINITION: Showing consideration for others; mannerly. Refined; cultured.

MONDAY: The trait of the week is politeness. Polite is defined as having or exhibiting good manners. A person who is polite is courteous. They think of others before acting or speaking. You will often hear polite words like thank you, may I, excuse me, please, you're welcome. Polite people use a courteous tone of voice. Today, talk about things you can do to show politeness in your classroom.

TUESDAY: The trait of the week is politeness. Polite is defined as having or exhibiting good manners. Being thoughtful is the first rule of being polite. Today we are going to accent the words "Thank you." These are polite words because they let the other person know you appreciate and value the good they bring to your life. Today use every chance you have to say, "Thank you."

WEDNESDAY: The trait of the week is politeness. Polite is defined as having or exhibiting good manners. Today we are going to talk about the word "PLEASE." This word is a short way of saying 'if you please.' It gives another person the right and power to say 'yes' ' or 'no'. To please someone is to make them happy…so when we say 'please' we are really asking, "Will this make you happy to do for me…or give to me? Today practice using the polite term 'please'.

THURSDAY: The trait of the week is politeness. Polite is defined as having or exhibiting good manners. We live in a crowded world. From time to time we are going to bump into someone, or need to interrupt them as they speak. The polite words to use when this happens are "Excuse me, please." These three little words can keep an accidental bump from turning to a vicious fight. Use them today and see how they work for you!

FRIDAY: The trait of the week is politeness. Polite is defined as having or exhibiting good manners. Being polite is not difficult, but it does take some thought. Polite people are welcomed anywhere. They are respected for their good manners. All of us need to develop polite behaviors and make them habits in our life. The key is to think of the other person before you think or act. One of the nice compliments that we can receive at (name of school) is when a guest says our students and staff are so polite and courteous.

Thoughts to Ponder:

"Politeness in an individual is as necessary as paint on both sides of a fence, for a person, like a fence, faces out as well as in."

Marcelene Cox

"A meal in pleasant company benefits the heart as well as the body."

Proverb

"It is not sufficient to know what one ought to say, but one must also know how to say it."

Aristotle

"We can always oblige, but we can always speak obligingly."

Voltaire

"Pleasant words are honey on the tongue and music to the ear."

Old proverb

Suggested Books:

Saying I'm Sorry, Laura Alden

Eddycat Introduces Mannersville, Ada Barnett, Pam Manquen and Linda Rapaport

Eddycat Teaches Telephone Skills, Ada Barnett, Pam Manquen and Linda Rapaport

The Manners Book, June Behrens

The Berenstain Bears Forget Their Manners, Stan and Jan Berenstain

Let's Talk About Being Rude, Joy Wilt Berry

Perfect Pigs, An Introduction to Manners, Marc Brown and Stephen Krensky

Pass the Fritters, Critters, Cheryl Chapman

Dinner at Alberta's, Russell Hoban

The Muppet Guide to Magnificent Manners, James Howe

What Do You Say, Dear?, Sesyle Joslin

Saying Please, Jane Belk Moncure

Please...Thanks...I'm Sorry!, Jane Belk Moncure

Manners, Shelly Nielsen

Mind Your Manners, Peggy Parrish

"EXCUSE ME," Janet Riehecky

"I'M SORRY," Janet Riehecky

"AFTER YOU," Janet Riehecky

"THANK YOU," Janet Riehecky

Please and Thank You Book, Richard Scarry

Excuse Me! Certainly, Louis Slobodkin

Excuse Me, You're Standing in Front of the TV, Karen Romano Young

Excuse Me, May I Have an Extra Napkin?, Karen Romano Young

Please, May I Have a Pencil?, Karen Romano Young

Please Come to My Party, Karen Romano Young

Excuse Me, But It's My Turn, Karen Romano Young

(For a complete annotated listing of these books see the bibliography, page 91.)

Truthfulness

DEFINITION: Habitually telling the truth; a truthful person. Faithful to truth or to the facts.

MONDAY: The trait of the week is truthfulness. To be truthful means to be faithful to the facts; saying and doing what is honest. We are not perfect people—sometimes we make wrong decisions about our behavior. When that happens, being honest or truthful is the best way to "make things right." First of all, we must be truthful with ourselves and admit we did not make a good choice. Then, we must be truthful with whomever we have wronged and take the responsibility and consequence of our wrong decision.

TUESDAY: The trait of the week is truthfulness. To be truthful means to be faithful to the facts, saying and doing what is honest. Today, I would like you to imagine this situation: You are home and you are bored, so you decided to borrow your sister's boom box without asking. On the way downstairs, you drop it and break it. What would be the truthful way to handle this situation.

WEDNESDAY: The trait of the week is truthfulness. To be truthful means to be faithful to the facts, saying and doing what is honest. Being truthful means to tell a story factually; the way it really happened. Today, I would like for you to discuss how being truthful helps us when we have made wrong decision.

THURSDAY: The trait of the week is truthfulness. To be truthful means to be faithful to the facts, saying and doing what is honest. You stop to buy ice cream on your way home from school. The clerk is new and confused, he gives you back too much change. Are you going to do the truthful thing and tell the clerk, or pocket the money for the ice cream tomorrow? Discuss in your class the honest thing to do.

FRIDAY: The trait of the week is truthfulness. To be truthful means to be faithful to the facts, saying and doing what is honest. Abraham Lincoln once asked, "How many legs does a sheep have if you call its tail a leg?" The person being questioned answered, "Five," "No", said Mr. Lincoln, "calling a tail a leg does not make it one. The sheep still has only four legs." Make sure you are growing the character it takes to be known as a truthful person.

Thoughts to Ponder:

"Truth is always the strongest argument."

Sophocles

"No one has a good enough memory to be a successful liar."

Abraham Lincoln

"This is the punishment of the liar; he is not believed, even when he speaks speaks the truth."

The Talmud

"Falsehood not only disagree with truths, but usually quarrel among themselves."

Daniel Webster

"Things are never quite the same somehow after you have to lie to a person."

Christopher Morley

Suggested Books:

Diogenes, Aliki

The Emperor's New Clothes, Hans Christian Anderson

The Bird, the Frog, and the Light, Avi

Let's Talk about Cheating, Joy Wilt Berry

The Berenstain Bears and the Truth, Stan and Jan Berenstain

Wishful Lying, Rose Blue

The True Francine, Marc Brown

Arnie and the Stolen Markers, Nancy Carlson

Harriet and the Garden, Nancy Carlson

The Empty Pot, Demi

Ernie's Little Lie, Dan Elliot

Rabbit Rambles On, Susanna Gretz

Jamacia's Find, Juantia Havill

Honesty: What Is It?, Janet Belk Moncure

Who Was It?, Marissa Moss

Telling the Truth, Shelley Nielsen

A Big Fat Enormous Lie, Marjorie Sharmat

(For a complete annotated listing of these books see the bibliography, page 88.)

Honesty

DEFINITION: The condition or quality of being honest; acting honorably and justly; not lying, stealing or cheating.

MONDAY: The trait of the week is honesty. Honesty means acting honorably and justly, not lying, stealing or cheating. Are you honest and truthful? Do you lie or always tell the whole truth. Discuss in your class this saying, "A half-truth is a whole lie".

TUESDAY: The trait of the week is honesty. Honesty means acting honorably and justly, not lying, stealing or cheating. Honesty is a character trait that is valued in all cultures. Just because it is universally worthy does not mean that it is easy. Today, discuss this saying, "The truth is best not spoken at all times".

WEDNESDAY: The trait of the week is honesty. Honesty means acting honorably and justly, not lying, stealing or cheating. The 16th President of our country was sometimes called "Honest Abe." One reason why he earned that name is this. He borrowed a book from the lending library that would come to town every few months. Lincoln lived in a log cabin and had to sleep in the loft. He liked to read at night. One night, due to rain storm, the book he had borrowed got wet. He worked very hard chopping and selling wood so that he could pay for the damaged book. When the horse and buggy came carrying the 'Lending Library" Lincoln paid for the book. Discuss the qualities that made him "Honest Abe".

THURSDAY: The trait of the week is honesty. Honesty means acting honorably and justly, not lying, stealing or cheating. Billy wants to see a movie. He has no money. Mother was saving some money in the cookie jar for Dad's birthday gift. Billy reached for the cookie jar with mix feeling of guilt and anticipation. What do you think Billy will do? What do you think he should do? Discuss this in your classroom.

FRIDAY: The trait of the week is honesty. Honesty means acting honorably and justly, not lying, stealing or cheating. This week we've learned that honesty is a matter of 'doing' the truth as well as 'speaking' the truth. Today draw a picture showing an example of someone 'doing' something honest. Take it home. Show your family and tell them what you learned this week about being honest.

Thoughts to Ponder:

"A liar begins with making falsehood appear like truth, and ends with making truth appear like falsehood."

William Shenstone

"A lie has always a certain amount of weight with those who wish to believe it."

Elliot W. Rice

"Fiction has its own kind of truth. It can be real without being factual."

Author unknown

"A half-truth is a whole lie."

Author unknown

"A man that seeks truth and loves it must be reckoned precious to any society."

Frederick the Great

Suggested Books:

Diogenes, Aliki

The Emperor's New Clothes, Hans Christian Anderson

The Bird, the Frog, and the Light, Avi

Let's Talk about Cheating, Joy Wilt Berry

The Berenstain Bears and the Truth, Stan and Jan Berenstain

Wishful Lying, Rose Blue

The True Francine, Marc Brown

Arnie and the Stolen Markers, Nancy Carlson

Harriet and the Garden, Nancy Carlson

The Emply Pot, Demi

Ernie's Little Lie, Dan Elliot

Rabbit Rambles On, Susanna Gretz

Jamacia's Find, Juantia Havill

Honesty: What Is It?, Janet Belk Moncure

Who Was It?, Marissa Moss

Telling the Truth, Shelley Nielsen

A Big Fat Enormous Lie, Marjorie Sharmat

(For a complete annotated listing of these books see the bibliography, page 88.)

Kindness

DEFINITION: The condition or quality of being kind; willing to help; gentle; friendly; sympathetic.

MONDAY: The trait of the week is kindness. Kindness means to be gentle, willing to help, friendly and considerate. Today, let's talk about kind words. I would like for you to list some words or phrases that convey kindness. I'll get you started with an easy one—I'm sorry. Spend a few minutes expanding that list.

TUESDAY: The trait of the week is kindness. Kindness means to be gentle, willing to help, friendly and considerate. There is a very easy way to decide if what we are going to do or say is kind. All we have to do is ask ourselves; is that what I would like someone to say or do to me? Discuss this idea in your class.

WEDNESDAY: The trait of the week is kindness. Kindness is to be gentle, willing to help, friendly and considerate. Some people have mistaken that it is a sign of weakness to be gentle and kind. This is not true! It takes much self-control not to answer a harsh remark in the same way. It is a mark of true strength to give back kindness when a hurtful answer seems to be right. Today be strong enough to be kind. Make your words sweet today.

THURSDAY: The trait of the week is kindness. Kindness is to be gentle, willing to help, friendly and considerate. When you see someone who needs a helping hand and you give it you are being kind. Many of the students who have earned Good Citizens awards have earned them by being helpful. Like helping someone who has dropped their tray for example. Discuss ways that you can be helpful at home or at school. Remember, every time you are helpful, you are being kind.

FRIDAY: The trait of the week is kindness. Kindness is to gentle, willing to help, friendly and considerate. This week we have focused on the character trait of kindness. We hope that it will become a part of you. There is a test to help you decide if what you are to say or do is right. Ask yourself: Is it kind? Is it true? Is it helpful? Unless you can answer "yes" to these three questions don't say or do it.

Thoughts to Ponder:

"Kindness is the oil that takes the friction out of life."

Author unknown

"If everyone gives a thread, the poor man will have a shirt."

Russian proverb

"A wise person hears one words and understand two."

Proverb

"When you stop to think, don't forget to start again."

Author unknown

"The way something is given is worth more than the gift itself."

French proverb

Suggested Books:

Home in the Sky, Jeannie Baker

After Dark, Louis Baum

The Owl Who Loved Sunshine, Mary Carey

Penrod's Party, Mary Blount Christian

T.J. Flopp, Stephen Cosgrove

Osa's Pride, Ann Grifalconi

Jennie's Hat, Ezra Jack Keats

Caring: What Is It?, Jane Belk Moncure

Caring, Shelly Neilsen

They're Only Words, Deborah Testi

The Lazy Bear, Brian Wildsmith

(For a complete annotated listing of these books see the bibliography, page 84.)

Thankfulness

DEFINITION:
To express gratitude to; give thanks.

MONDAY: The trait of the week is thankfulness. To be thankful means to express gratitude, or to give thanks. Thankfulness is such an important trait that our country have set aside a day for counting all the reasons we have to be thankful. Even if we don't have fancy turkey dinner with all the trimmings, we can be thankful that we have the appetite for it!

TUESDAY: The trait of the week is thankfulness. To be thankful means to express gratitude, or to give thanks. Today discuss with your classmates the people you are thankful for. For example, I am thankful for my family, for all they do for me. I am truly grateful for having them.

WEDNESDAY: The trait of the week is thankfulness. To be thankful means to express gratitude, or to give thanks. Yesterday we discussed the people you are thankful for knowing or sharing your life with. Everyone has special talents. Today, make a list of these special talents you are thankful to have. For example; I am thankful for being able to sing. What are your talents you are thankful for?

THURSDAY: The trait of the week is thankfulness. To be thankful means to express gratitude, or to give thanks. We have discussed the people we are thankful for and the talents we have. Today, let us discuss the things at school you are thankful for. Example—I am thankful for the books to read at school.

FRIDAY: The trait of the week is thankfulness. To be thankful means to express gratitude, or to give thanks. This week we talked about thankfulness. Saying "thank you" is a polite thing to do. It let the other person know that you appreciate what they have done for you. Practice today saying the words "thank you" in as many different ways as you can think. Perhaps you can even sing them, or write a poem.

Thoughts to Ponder:

"There is as much greatness of mind in acknowledging a good turn, as in doing it."

Senecca

"For health and strength and daily bread, we give thanks today."

Old Song

"Appreciation not expressed is like a good book which is left unread."

Author unknown

"Blessed are those who can give without remembering, and take without forgetting."

Elizabeth Bibesco

"Unshared joy is an unlighted candle."

Spanish proverb

Suggested Books:

Hush Little Baby: A Folk Lullaby, Aliki

Fox and Heggie, Sandra E. Guzzo

I'm Thankful Each Day!, P.K. Hallinan

Tico and the Golden Wings, Leo Lionni

Thankfulness, Janet McDonnell

I Never Say I'm Thankful, But I Am, Janet Belk Moncure

If You Give a Moose a Muffin, Laura Joffe Numeroff

Aesops Fables, Tom Paxton

Andocles and the Lion, and Other Aesops' Fables, Tom Paxton

Saying Thank You, Colleen L. Reece

"Thank You," Janet Riehecky

A Chair for My Mother, Vera B. Williams

The Banza, Diane Wolkstein

(For a complete annotated listing of these books see the bibliography, page 87.)

Generosity

DEFINITION:
The quality of being generous. A generous act.

MONDAY: The trait of the week is generosity. Generosity is the quality of being generous; a generous act. We live in a world where kindness is always rewarded. When you help someone, you will usually receive many thanks from others for your kindness. When we truly give generously, we give without asking for anything in return. What act of generosity will you perform today?

TUESDAY: The trait of the week is generosity. Generosity is the quality of being generous; a generous act. Write in your journal today about a service or act of kindness you may have shown to someone else.

WEDNESDAY: The trait of the week is generosity. Generosity is the quality of being generous; a generous act. Sometimes the act of generosity involves a personal sacrifice. You may have to give up something you value to help someone else. Some people have donated one of their organs to benefit others. Discuss in your class things that you would be willing to sacrifice for the benefit of others.

THURSDAY: The trait of the week is generosity. Generosity is the quality of being generous; a generous act. James and Erica are very good friends and have been for a long time. You notice that Erica is never generous with her things. If you were James, how would you encourage her to be more generous and giving? Write your response in your journal.

FRIDAY: The trait of the week is generosity. Generosity is the quality of being generous; a generous act. Generosity is an act of unconditional love for another. How have you demonstrated generosity this week? How do feel about the generosity you have shown to others?

Thoughts to Ponder:

"The dead take to the grave, clutched in their hands, only what they have given away."

DeWitt Wallace

"When you decide to give yourself to a great cause, you must arrive at the point where no sacrifice is too great."

Coretta Scott King

"A man does not have to be an angel in order to be a saint."

Albert Schweitzer

"I just wanted to make a difference, however small, in the world."

Arthur Ashe

"A sure way for one to lift himself up is by helping to lift someone else."

Booker T. Washington

Suggested Books:

Hush Little Baby: A Folk Lullaby, Aliki

Fox and Heggie, Sandra E. Guzzo

I'm Thankful Each Day!, P.K. Hallinan

Tico and the Golden Wings, Leo Lionni

Thankfulness, Janet McDonnell

I Never Say I'm Thankful, But I Am, Janet Belk Moncure

If You Give a Moose a Muffin, Laura Joffe Numeroff

Aesops Fables, Tom Paxton

Andocles and the Lion, and Other Aesops' Fables, Tom Paxton

Saying Thank You, Colleen L. Reece

"Thank You," Janet Riehecky

A Chair for My Mother, Vera B. Williams

The Banza, Diane Wolkstein

(For a complete annotated listing of these books see the bibliography, page 87.)

Goodwill

DEFINITION: Having good feelings toward others; gaining a good reputation and friendly relationship between a business and its customers.

MONDAY: The trait of the week is goodwill. Goodwill is having good feelings towards others and gaining a good reputation between a business and its customers. John and Jeffrey are best friends and have been since first grade. John needs to buy paper and pencils for school but does not have any money. Jeffrey knows that John needs the school supplies so he buys them for John with his birthday money. Weeks pass and Jeffrey never receives money from John for the supplies. Jeffrey never mentions the money to John and still considers John his best friend. How has Jeffrey demonstrated goodwill?

TUESDAY: The trait of the week is goodwill. Goodwill is having good feelings towards others and gaining a good reputation between a business and its customers. Mother Teresa spent the majority of her life living with and loving people who lived in poverty-stricken countries. She saved the lives of many young children simply by lovingly touching them. She knew that research had proven that the human touch helps the body release certain chemicals that help the body to live and grow. How has Mother Teresa demonstrated goodwill? How can you demonstrate goodwill?

WEDNESDAY: The trait of the week is goodwill. Goodwill is having good feelings towards others and gaining a good reputation between a business and its customers. Positive thoughts can be very powerful. Things that are thought to be impossible become possible through the power of positive thinking. You can demonstrate goodwill just by thinking good thoughts about someone. As a demonstration of goodwill, think positive thoughts about someone today.

THURSDAY: The trait of the week is goodwill. Goodwill is having good feelings towards others and gaining a good reputation between a business and its customers. Think of ways that your actions can demonstrate goodwill. Look around you and you will find many opportunities (in your home, school or community) to demonstrate goodwill. How can you use your skills and talents to help others around you?

FRIDAY: The trait of the week is goodwill. Goodwill is having good feelings towards others and gaining a good reputation between a business and its customers. When you truly care about others, there are no strings attached to your giving. You don't expect to receive anything in return for your act of kindness. When you demonstrate goodwill, you give or serve for free without expecting anything back. What gift or service will you offer without getting anything in return?

Thoughts to Ponder:

"I have found the paradox that if I love until it hurts, then there is no hurt, but only more love."

Mother Teresa

"Someone's got to go out there and love people and show it."

Diana, the late Princess of Wales

"Love builds..."

Mary McLeod Bethune (Founder and president of Bethune-Cookman College)

"Friends are my heart and my ears."

Michael Jordan

"Ask not what your country can do for you—ask what you can do for your country."

John F. Kennedy

Suggested Books:

Fish and Flamingo, Nancy White Carlstrom

Great Kapok Tree, Lynne Cherry

Watch Out for Chicken Feet in Your Soup, Tomie De Paola

Are You My Friend?, Janice Derby

Respect, Beverly Fiday and Deborah Crowdy

Good Morning, Good Night, Ivan Gantschev

Just About Perfect, Kate Green

The Lady and the Spider, Faith NcNutly

Cocoon, Diane Redfield Massie

The Porcupine Mouse, Bonnie Pryor

Python's Party, Brian Wildsmith

(For a complete annotated listing of these books see the bibliography, page 83.)

Joyfulness

DEFINITION:
A strong feeling of happiness, contentment, or satisfaction

MONDAY: The trait of the week is joyfulness. Joyfulness means to have a strong feeling of happiness, contentment, or satisfaction. Make a list today of all the things that bring you a great deal of joy. Compare your list with others. Discuss ways that you can bring the feeling of joy to others.

TUESDAY: The trait of the week is joyfulness. Joyfulness means to have a strong feeling of happiness, contentment, or satisfaction. Discuss in your classrooms today the following: Would you rather spend your day with a person who is cheerful and full of joy or a person who is negative and full of gloom?

WEDNESDAY: The trait of the week is joyfulness. Joyfulness means to have a strong feeling of happiness, contentment, or satisfaction. Have you ever spent time around a person that was full of joy and happiness? They are like human battery chargers. They energize others. You too can be a human energizer. Start by refusing to say negative things. Bite your tongue, count to ten! When you send out positive words, thoughts and feelings, positive people are attracted to you!

THURSDAY: The trait of the week is joyfulness. Joyfulness means to have a strong feeling of happiness, contentment, or satisfaction. When you do something silly (everyone does), don't miss the opportunity to laugh at yourself. It's one of life's great joys! If you laugh a lot you'll be healthier. Laughter releases good chemicals in your body that help you grow.

FRIDAY: The trait of the week is joyfulness. Joyfulness means to have a strong feeling of happiness, contentment, or satisfaction. Greet each new day with excitement! Approach your tasks today with energy and enthusiasm. Joyfulness is catching. Demonstrating this trait can help you win friends and gain the respect of others.

Thoughts to Ponder:

"Grief can take care of itself; but to get the full value of joy you must have somebody to divide it with."

Mark Twain

"You are the only one who can grade your life, so give yourself an A+."

Deborah Stein

"He who laughs, lasts."

Anonymous

"Laughter softens life's rough edges."

Cherie Carter-Scott

"Humor and laughter are tremendously important in relationships. Sharing a good laugh with someone does wonders for the soul."

Anonymous

Suggested Books:

The Sheep and the Rowan Tree, Julia Butcher

Life Is Fun!, Nancy Carlson

I Like Me!, Nancy Carlson

Across the Blue Mountains, Emma Chichester Clark

Shine, Sun!, Carol Greene

Away Go the Boats, Margaret Hillert

A Time for Singing, Ron Hirshi

Miranda's Smile, Thomas Locker

Happy Hiding Hippos, Bobette McCarthy

JOY: What Is It?, Jane Belk Moncure

"Smile," Says Little Crocodile, Jane Belk Moncure

The Happy Owls, Celestina Piatti

Sun Jack and Rain Jack, Ursel Scheffler

I Am Not a Crybaby, Norma Simon

Spinky Sulks, William Steig

The Lady Who Saw the Good in Everything, Pat Decker Tapio

The Clown's Smile, Mike Thaler

Smile Ernest and Celestine, Gabrielle Vincent

The Happy Hedgehog Band, Martin Waddell

Rock Finds a Friend, Randall J. Wiethorn

(For a complete annotated listing of these books see the bibliography, page 94.)

Patience

DEFINITION:
The condition or quality of being patient; the ability to wait.

MONDAY: The trait of the week is patience. Patience is the condition or quality of being patient or demonstrating the ability to wait. Thomas Jefferson, 3rd President of the United States once said, "Delay is preferable to error". What does this statement tell you about the way Thomas Jefferson made decisions? Do you think his attitude of patience contributed towards the greatness of the Declaration of Independence?

TUESDAY: The trait of the week is patience. Patience is the condition or quality of being patient or demonstrating the ability to wait. Danielle was very anxious to finish her test so that she could go to recess. She quickly answered all of the questions and got up to turn her test paper in. Her teacher explained that she should always read back through her work to check for any errors or mistakes. Danielle just knew that all of her answers were correct because she had studied the night before. As Danielle looked over her answers, she realized that she had left one whole page blank!! In her haste she had skipped over a page. Danielle completed the blank page and turned her test in. She promised herself that she would take her time and exercise more patience in the future.

WEDNESDAY: The trait of the week is patience. Patience is the condition or quality of being patient or demonstrating the ability to wait. Discuss in your classroom today a time when you did not demonstrate patience. Did you achieve the results you wanted? What have you learned from that lesson?

THURSDAY: The trait of the week is patience. Patience is the condition or quality of being patient or demonstrating the ability to wait. As a young student, you need to wait until you're old enough for certain things you want to have and do—buy a car, get your own apartment, stay up late. You are exercising patience by waiting to do these things. How have some of the adults in your life demonstrated patience? Do all people have to exercise patience at some time in their life?

FRIDAY: The trait of the week is patience. Patience is the condition or quality of being patient or demonstrating the ability to wait. You have had many opportunities to demonstrate patience throughout the week. Share with the class times that you have demonstrated patience this week.

Thoughts to Ponder:

"One thing today, another tomorrow."

Spanish Proverb

"Be patient. You'll know when it's time for you to wake up and move ahead."

Ram Das

"Learning is not attained by chance, it must be sought for with ardor and attended to with diligence."

Abigail Adams (Former First Lady)

"Genius is one percent inspiration and ninety-nine percent perspiration."

Thomas Alva Edison

"A stitch in time saves nine."

English Proverb

Suggested Books:

D.W. Flips!, Marc Brown
See How They Grow: Kittens, Jane Burton and Angela Royston
The Waiting Day, Harriet Diller
Good As New, Barbara Douglass
Patience, What Is It?, Beverly Fiday
Once Around the Block, Kevin Henkes

Grandma Gets Grumpy, Anna Grossnickle Hines
Not Yet, Yvette, Mary Kettleman
Leo the Late Bloomer, Robert Kraus
Little Things, Anne Laurin
Is It Bedtime?, Dave Ross
Max's Breakfast, Rosemary Wells

(For a complete annotated listing of these books see the bibliography, page 81.)

Cooperation

DEFINITION:
A working together for a common purpose; a joint action.

MONDAY: The trait of the week is cooperation. Cooperation is working together for a common purpose or a joint action. Share with the class a situation when you accomplished more by working with another person than by working alone.

TUESDAY: The trait of the week is cooperation. Cooperation is working together for a common purpose or a joint action. Symbiosis is the state where two unlike organisms live together in a benefiting relationship to both. How are cooperation and symbiosis alike and how are they different?

WEDNESDAY: The trait of the week is cooperation. Cooperation is working together for a common purpose or a joint action. Crucial or critical cooperation is defined as cooperation that is necessary to the survival of two individuals or groups of individuals. Where in our society can you find an example of crucial or critical cooperation. Share your examples with the class.

THURSDAY: The trait of the week is cooperation. Cooperation is working together for a common purpose or a joint action. It has been said that, "support is the fuel that keeps you going when you want to stop". You can demonstrate the trait cooperation through your support. How have you demonstrated support and cooperation towards others?

FRIDAY: The trait of the week is cooperation. Cooperation is working together for a common purpose or a joint action. Discuss with the class a person that you feel demonstrates cooperation. How does/did that person demonstrate cooperation?

Thoughts to Ponder:

"One hand can not applaud."

Arabian Proverb

"If everyone pitched in, where would all the problems go?"

Anonymous

"Two heads are better than one."

Proverb

"I don't believe in just ordering people to do things. You have to grab an oar and row with them."

Harold Geneen

"A sure way for one to lift himself up is by helping to lift someone else."

Booker T. Washington

Suggested Books:

Helping Out, George Acona

The Grandpa Days, Joan W. Blos

Not Like That, Like This!, Tony Bradman and Joanna Burroughes

HELPING: What Is It? Jane Buerger

It Takes a Village, Jane Cowen-Fletcher

At Taylor's Place, Sharon Phillips Denslow

It's Easy, Deborah Hautzig

Alfie Gives a Hand, Shirley Hughes

Frog and Toad Together, Arnold Lobel

Bizzy Bones and the Lost Quilt, Jacqueline Briggs Martin

Helpful Betty to the Rescue, Michaela Morgan

Helpful Betty Solves a Mystery, Michaela Morgan

Cooperation, Values to Live By, Janey Riehecky

Stone Soup, Tony Ross

Two and Too Much, Mildred Pitts Walter

Elephant and Crocodile, Max Valthuijs

(For a complete annotated listing of these books see the bibliography, page 93.)

Tolerance

DEFINITION: An attitude toward others which is fair and free from emotional bias regardless of differences in beliefs, customs, or race.

MONDAY: The trait of the week is tolerance. Tolerance is having an attitude toward others which is fair and free from bias. Have you ever had a preconceived idea about a person or group, then found out you were wrong once you got to know them? Discuss with your class a time when you were tolerant of another.

TUESDAY: The trait of the week is tolerance. Tolerance is having an attitude toward others which is fair and free from bias. It has been said that the more you learn the less you fear. Once you learn that you have nothing to fear you become more willing to try more new things, ideas, and relationships. You become more tolerant of other people's opinions and beliefs. How will you show tolerance today?

WEDNESDAY: The trait of the week is tolerance. Tolerance is having an attitude toward others which is fair and free from bias. The more people you know, especially those who are different from you, the more interesting your life becomes. What if all your friends looked, thought, and behaved exactly alike? How interesting would your life be? Write in your journal your thoughts and ideas about the importance of diversity in our lives.

THURSDAY: The trait of the week is tolerance. Tolerance is having an attitude toward others which is fair and free from bias. Don't ever judge a whole group of people by one person's action. Doing so can lead to prejudice and discrimination. How can you show fairness by not judging others harshly?

FRIDAY: The trait of the week is tolerance. Tolerance is having an attitude toward others which is fair and free from bias. As we are learning about our differences, look also at our similarities. You probably have more in common than you know. Write in your journals about a friend of yours who is different from you but also has a lot in common with you.

Thoughts to Ponder:

*"He drew a circle that shut me out—Heretic, rebel, a thing to flout.
But Love and I had the wit to win; We drew a circle that took him in!"*

Edward Markham

"With compassion, we see benevolently our own human condition and the condition of our fellow beings. We drop prejudice. We withhold judgement."

Christina Baldwin

"I accept the universe!"

Margaret Fuller

"All life is interrelated. The agony of the poor impoverished the rich; the betterment of the poor enriches the rich. Whatever affects one directly affects all indirectly."

Dr. Martin Luther King Jr.

"In celebrating ethnic differences we often discover how much people are really the same. People are people. They all have feelings."

Tomie de Paola

Suggested Books:

Fish and Flamingo, Nancy White Carlstrom

Great Kapok Tree, Lynne Cherry

Watch Out for Chicken Feet in Your Soup, Tomie De Paola

Are You My Friend?, Janice Derby

Respect, Beverly Fiday and Deborah Crowdy

Good Morning, Good Night, Ivan Gantschev

Just About Perfect, Kate Green

The Lady and the Spider, Faith NcNutly

Cocoon, Diane Redfield Massie

The Porcupine Mouse, Bonnie Pryor

Python's Party, Brian Wildsmith

(For a complete annotated listing of these books see the bibliography, page 83.)

Consideration

DEFINITION: The action of thinking carefully; thoughtful concern; as for the feelings or interests of others.

MONDAY: The trait of the week is consideration. Consideration is the action of thinking carefully and showing thoughtful concern for the interest and feelings of others. With your words and actions you can demonstrate consideration for others. Discuss with your class things you can do to demonstrate consideration.

TUESDAY: The trait of the week is consideration. Consideration is the action of thinking carefully and showing thoughtful concern for the interest and feelings of others. Sometimes the kindest words are those that aren't spoken. How can you demonstrate consideration by not spreading rumors, gossiping, or telling cruel stories about others?

WEDNESDAY: The trait of the week is consideration. Consideration is the action of thinking carefully and showing thoughtful concern for the interest and feelings of others. Pretend you are the friend of a person who doesn't know how to share and does not care about the feelings of others. How might you encourage your friend to show consideration to others?

THURSDAY: The trait of the week is consideration. Consideration is the action of thinking carefully and showing thoughtful concern for the interest and feelings of others. Make a conscious effort today to show consideration. Write in your journal the ways you plan to demonstrate consideration for others.

FRIDAY: The trait of the week is consideration. Consideration is the action of thinking carefully and showing thoughtful concern for the interest and feelings of others. Share with the class through your journal writings the ways that you demonstrated the trait consideration this week.

Thoughts to Ponder:

"The way in which something is given is worth more than the gift itself."

French Proverb

"You can't understand another person until you walk a few miles in their moccasins."

Native American Proverb

"There is a magnet in your heart that will attract true friends. That magnet is unselfishness, thinking of others first...when you learn to live for others, they will live for you."

Paramahansa Yogananda

"Supporting another means giving with no agenda."

Anonymous

"A sure way for one to lift himself up is by helping to lift someone else."

Booker T. Washington

Suggested Books:

Home in the Sky, Jeannie Baker
After Dark, Louis Baum
The Owl Who Loved Sunshine, Mary Carey
Penrod's Party, Mary Blount Christian
T.J. Flopp, Stephen Cosgrove
Osa's Pride, Ann Grifalconi

Jennie's Hat, Ezra Jack Keats
Caring: What Is It?, Jane Belk Moncure
Caring, Shelly Neilsen
They're Only Words, Deborah Testi
The Lazy Bear, Brian Wildsmith

(For a complete annotated listing of these books see the bibliography, page 84.)

Uniqueness

DEFINITION:
Being the only one of its type; without an equal or like; singular.

MONDAY: The trait of the week is uniqueness. Uniqueness means to be the only one of its type; having no equal. Everyone of us is unique. There is not another person exactly like you in the world. Write down all the special things about yourself that make you unique. Share your list with your class.

TUESDAY: The trait of the week is uniqueness. Uniqueness means to be the only one of its type; having no equal. Jeffrey and Brian are identical twins. They do everything together. They both play basketball, soccer, and baseball and are on each other's teams. One day, Jeffrey told Brian that he would like to take piano lessons. Brian said that taking piano lessons would be the last thing on earth he would want to do. Brian suggested that they both take tennis lessons. Discuss with your classmates if you think Jeffrey should go ahead and take piano lessons by himself or take tennis lessons with his brother.

WEDNESDAY: The trait of the week is uniqueness. Uniqueness means to be the only one of its type; having no equal. To be unique does not mean that you have to be perfect. Even though you are not perfect you are still a unique and wonderful person with many strong positive character traits. What are some of your positive character traits that make you unique?

THURSDAY: The trait of the week is uniqueness. Uniqueness means to be the only one of its type; having no equal. When you are aware of your unique skills, abilities, and interests you can be more confident and accepting of yourself and others. How does taking pride in those things that make you unique help you be a stronger more confident person? Write your response in your journal.

FRIDAY: The trait of the week is uniqueness. Uniqueness means to be the only one of its type; having no equal. Discuss this quote by Paula P. Brownlee, "To do good things in the world, first you must know who you are and what gives meaning in your life." How does this quote relate to the character trait uniqueness.

Thoughts to Ponder:

"Every person is an unrepeatable miracle."

Anonymous

"Every man has his peculiar ambition."

Abraham Lincoln

"Each human is uniquely different. Like snowflakes, the human pattern is never cast twice."

Alice Childress

"I just wanted to be somebody. I always assumed I would be."

Natalie Babbitt

"To do things in the world, first you must know who you are and what gives meaning to your life."

Paula P. Brownlee

Suggested Books:

The Story of Johnny Appleseed, Aliki

The Owl Who Loved Sunshine, Mary Carey

The Value of Believing in Yourself: The Story of Louis Pasteur, Spencer Johnson

Someday, Said Mitchell, Barbara Williams

(For a complete annotated listing of these books see the bibliography, page 100.)

Patriotism

DEFINITION:
Love of one's country and loyal devotion to it.

MONDAY: The trait of the week is patriotism. Patriotism means to love one's country with loyalty and devotion. Nathan Hale was quoted as saying, "I regret that I have but one life to give to my country." Based on this statement, discuss in your classroom if you think Nathan Hale demonstrated patriotism.

TUESDAY: The trait of the week is patriotism. Patriotism means to love one's country with loyalty and devotion. When we say the Pledge of Allegiance, we are pledging our loyalty to our country. How can students demonstrate love and loyal devotion to our country? Write your response in your journal.

WEDNESDAY: The trait of the week is patriotism. Patriotism means to love one's country with loyalty and devotion. If you could go back in time and meet the patriot Nathan Hale and discuss what America meant to him, what do you think he would say? Are there any patriots like Nathan Hale living today? Discuss this in your classroom.

THURSDAY: The trait of the week is patriotism. Patriotism means to love one's country with loyalty and devotion. Tanesha and Brittany read that United States Supreme Court Justice Sandra Day O'Connor has said that the 50 states are like small laboratories where people can create and develop ideas. What ideas can you create to make America a better country in which to live? Discuss these ideas in your classroom.

FRIDAY: The trait of the week is patriotism. Patriotism means to love one's country with loyalty and devotion. Former president, John F. Kennedy once said, "Ask not what your country can do for you, ask what you can do for your country." What did President Kennedy mean by this statement? Write your response in your journal.

Thoughts to Ponder:

"Ask not what your country can do for you—ask what you can do for your country."

John F. Kennedy

"The proper means of increasing the love we bear to our native land is to reside some time in a foreign one."

Anonymous

"I only regret that I have but one life to lose for my country."

Nathan Hale

Suggested Books:

Abe Lincoln's Hat, Martha Brenner

Wednesday's Surprise, Eve Bunting

Patriotic Fun, Judith Hoffman Corwin

Four Good Friends, Jock Curle

My First President's Day Book, Aileen Fisher

The Hole in the Dike, Norman Green

My First Fourth of July Book, Harriet Hodgson

Best Friends, Steven Kellog

The Inside-Outside Book of Washington, D.C., Roxie Munro

Legend of the Bluebonnet, Tomie DePaola

Grandfather's Journey, Allen Say

Arthur Sets Sail, Libor Schaffer

(For a complete annotated listing of these books see the bibliography, page 79.)

Citizenship

DEFINITION:
The condition of being a citizen, with all its rights and duties.

MONDAY: The trait of the week is citizenship. Citizenship means the condition of being a citizen with all its rights and duties. Citizenship is an action word. It means that we must do something to help out. How can students in your school demonstrate good citizenship? Discuss your response with the class.

TUESDAY: The trait of the week is citizenship. Citizenship means the condition of being a citizen with all its rights and duties. As a citizen you have some natural rights and duties. With these rights and duties come responsibilities. What responsibilities do you have as a citizen of the United States?

WEDNESDAY: The trait of the week is citizenship. Citizenship means the condition of being a citizen with all its rights and duties. Brainstorm in your classrooms ways that you can demonstrate good citizenship.

THURSDAY: The trait of the week is citizenship. Citizenship means the condition of being a citizen with all its rights and duties. Good citizens are caring, contributing, respectful people who obey laws and rules. How can you show good citizenship in your home and community? Journal your response.

FRIDAY: The trait of the week is citizenship. Citizenship means the condition of being a citizen with all its rights and duties. Good citizens are often patriotic. Write in your journals what you think it means to be a citizen of these United States. How do the laws of our country affect you?

Thoughts to Ponder:

"A person who neglects their duty as a citizen is not entitled to their rights as a citizen."

Author Unknown

"...democracy is not something you believe in, or a place you hang your hat, but it's something you do. You participate. If you stop doing it, democracy crumbles and falls apart."

Abbie Hoffman

"One has the right to be wrong in a democracy."

Claude Pepper

"The life of the nation is secure only while the nation is honest, truthful, and virtuous."

Frederick Douglass

"Never doubt that a small group of committed citizens can change the world. Indeed it is the only thing that ever has."

Margaret Mead

Suggested Books:

Who Keeps Us Safe?, Caroline Arnold

Wagon Wheels, Barbara Brenner

Safe Sally Seatbelt and the Magic Click, Phyliss Gobbell and Jim Laster

The Ox-Cart Man, Donald Hall

What If Everybody Did That?, Ellen Javernick

John Henry: An American Legend, Ezra Jack Keats

The Foxbury Force, Graham Oakley

Granny and the Desperadoes, Peggy Parish

Pleasant Pig and the Terrible Dragon, Richard Scarry

The Great Mystery Book, Richard Scarry

(For a complete annotated listing of these books see the bibliography, page 85.)

Loyalty

DEFINITION Faithful to one's country; constant and faithful to one's family, friends, or obligations.

MONDAY: The trait of the week is loyalty. Loyalty means to be faithful to one's country, family, friends, or obligations. When you are loyal to something or someone you are faithful and dependable. Imagine that you have a friend who is making some bad choices that could get him or her into serious trouble. Your friend has confided in you and has told you not to tell anyone. Your sense of loyalty tells you that you must tell her parents what you know, but your friend may see this as being disloyal and it could damage your friendship. What would you do? Discuss this with your class.

TUESDAY: The trait of the week is loyalty. Loyalty means to be faithful to one's country, family, friends, or obligations. You should be loyal to your parents and your family members even if you disagree with them or you think they are wrong about something. Are there any situations you can think of when it might be appropriate to be disloyal?

WEDNESDAY: The trait of the week is loyalty. Loyalty means to be faithful to one's country, family, friends, or obligations. A friend asks you to do something that's against the school rules. You know what he is asking you to do is wrong but, you don't want to lose his friendship. Should you do what he asks? Should you be loyal to your friend or to your school? What are the consequences of each choice? Write your responses in your journal.

THURSDAY: The trait of the week is loyalty. Loyalty means to be faithful to one's country, family, friends, or obligations. Make a list of all the things that require your loyalty; your school, your family, your community, your ideas. Rank order your list. Compare your list with your classmates. Are there any similarities or differences? Discuss them in your classroom.

FRIDAY: The trait of the week is loyalty. Loyalty means to be faithful to one's country, family, friends, or obligations. Practice being obedient for the whole day. Follow all of the necessary rules and procedures of your school. Write in your journal if this was an easy or difficult thing to accomplish.

Thoughts to Ponder:

"Ask not what your country can do for you, ask what you can do for your country."

John F. Kennedy

"Unless you can find some sort of loyalty, you cannot find unity and peace in your active living."

Josiah Royce

"When you're loyal to someone or something, you're faithful, constant, and dependable."

Anonymous

"I love my country. I feel good inside when I stand up and say the Pledge of Allegiance or sing "The Star Spangled Banner."

Ana Zavala

"When you decide to give yourself to a great cause, you must arrive at the point where no sacrifice is too great."

Suggested Books:

Abe Lincoln's Hat, Martha Brenner

Wednesday's Surprise, Eve Bunting

Patriotic Fun, Judith Hoffman Corwin

Four Good Friends, Jock Curle

My First President's Day Book, Aileen Fisher

The Hole in the Dike, Norman Green

My First Fourth of July Book, Harriet Hodgson

Best Friends, Steven Kellog

The Inside-Outside Book of Washington, D.C., Roxie Munro

Legend of the Bluebonnet, Tomie DePaola

Grandfather's Journey, Allen Say

Arthur Sets Sail, Libor Schaffer

(For a complete annotated listing of these books see the bibliography, page 79.)

Courage

DEFINITION:
The ability to meet danger or pain without giving in to fear.

MONDAY: The trait of the week is courage. Courage means to meet danger or pain without giving in to fear. It means doing the right thing even when it's scary or difficult. It means to try your best to succeed even when you are not guaranteed success. This week we will look at "Profiles in Courage", people who succeeded in spite of what others said was impossible. Tomorrow we will learn about courage shown by Sir Isaac Newton.

TUESDAY: The trait of the week is courage. Courage means to meet danger or pain without giving in to fear. Sir Isaac Newton was a very, very poor student in school. He was only allowed to stay in school because he was such a failure at farming. In spite of everything, Isaac grew up to become one of the most famous philosophers and mathematicians in history. Isaac Newton overcame his fears and turned failure into success.

WEDNESDAY: The trait of the week is courage. Courage means to meet danger or pain without giving in to fear. Rosa Parks was ordered to move to the back of the bus because she was black. She refused, forcing the police to remove, arrest, and put her in jail. The courage that Rosa showed to say "No" to racism sparked a boycott of the buses in Montgomery, Alabama. She became known as the mother of the American civil rights movement.

THURSDAY: The trait of the week is courage. Courage means to meet danger or pain without giving in to fear. Admiral Richard E. Byrd showed personal courage. He was retired by the Navy as being unfit for service. Although very hurt by this action, he was determined to prove them wrong. He became the legendary explorer who flew over the North Pole in 1926 and the South Pole in 1929.

FRIDAY: The trait of the week is courage. Courage means to meet danger or pain without giving in to fear. Our profiles in courage this week has shown us that people show courage in different ways. There are many ways that you can be courageous...standing up for someone who is being bullied by others; standing up in front of class and giving an oral report; coming back from a failure, or to continue to work hard even though you are tired and want to quit. It takes courage to learn and grow. Write in your journals how you will demonstrate courage in your life.

Thoughts to Ponder:

"Courage is the first of human qualities because it is the quality which guarantees all others."

Sir Winston Churchill

"Courage is doing what you're afraid to do. There can be no courage unless you're scared."

Eddie Rickenbacker

"You gain strength, courage and confidence by every experience in which you really stop to look fear in the face."

Eleanor Roosevelt

"One man with courage makes a majority."

Andrew Jackson

"Life shrinks or expands in proportion to one's courage."

Anais Nin

Suggested Books:

Joba and the Wild Boar, Gaby Balder

The Deep Dives of Stanley Whale, Nathaniel Benchley

Anna Banana and Me, Lenore Blegvad

Jim, Ruth Bornstein

Ghost's Hour, Spook's Hour, Eve Bunting

Harriet and the Roller Coaster, Nancy Carlson

My Brother John, Kristine Church

Eugene the Brave, Ellen Conford

The Polar Bear and the Brave Little Hare, Hans De Beers

Giant Story a Half Picture Book, Annegert Fuchshuber

Darkness and the Butterfly, Ann Grifalconi

The Great Diamond Robbery, Leon Garris

This Is the Bear and the Scary Night, Sarah Hayes and Helen Craig

Timothy Twinge, Florence Parry Jeide and Roxanne Heide Pierce

Arthur's Loose Tooth, Lillian Hoban

Brave Little Pete of Geranium Street, Rose and Samuel Lagercrantz

Friska the Sheep That Was Too Small, Rob Lewis

Jess Was the Brave One, Jean Little

The Boy Who Held Back the Sea, Thomas Locker

The Adventures of Isabel, Ogden Nath

Custard the Dragon, Ogden Nash

What Does It Mean AFRAID?, Susan Riley

Shy Charles, Rosemary Wells

(For a complete annotated listing of these books see the bibliography, page 85.)

Initiative

DEFINITION:
The first step in starting or doing something.

MONDAY: The trait of the week is initiative. Initiative means the first step in starting or doing something. You can show initiative by starting a job before you are asked to do it. You can also demonstrate this trait by taking the initiative to do extra work or assignments. Discuss how you can use initiative today at school.

TUESDAY: The trait of the week is initiative. Initiative means the first step in starting or doing something. Patricia's class was learning their multiplication facts for the fact families of 1, 2 and 3. Patricia learned those facts quickly. Then, without being asked she began memorizing her fact families for 4 and 5. Patricia's teacher told her, "Patricia, I am very impressed by you taking the initiative to learn extra facts! Great job!" Discuss how you think Patricia's initiative will help make her a better student.

WEDNESDAY: The trait of the week is initiative. Initiative means the first step in starting or doing something. Julie's teacher assigned a major report on one of the states. The teacher said, "Please break the project down into small steps. I suggest you choose a state, research it and then write your report." Julie was not excited about the project. She kept putting off making decisions. When it was time to turn the project in, Julie was not finished and received a bad grade. Discuss how taking the first step on the project could have helped Julie get a better grade.

THURSDAY: The trait of the week is initiative. Initiative means the first step in starting or doing something. The park by John's house needed clean up. There were broken bottles and trash every where. All the children who lived by the park complained about it, but no one did anything to fix the problem. On Monday, John started by the swings and cleaned up the area. On Tuesday he was working by the soccer fields and several children came over to help him. By Friday at least twenty children were working to clean up the park. Discuss how John's initiative brought about good changes for everyone.

FRIDAY: The trait of the week is initiative. Initiative means the first step in starting or doing something. Karl's mother was working late. When he got home he saw the dishwasher needed unloaded and the trash needed to be taken outside. Karl decided to surprise his mom and do both jobs before she got home. When his mother got home she was very surprised. She said, "Karl, I am so proud of you for helping out, without being asked!" Her compliments made Karl feel good. Using initiative can help others as well as yourself. Discuss how Karl was able to help others by taking the first step.

Thoughts to Ponder:

"The journey of a thousand miles starts with a single step."

Chinese proverb

"What saves a man is to take a step. Then another step. It is always the same step, but you have to take it."

Antoine de-Saint-Exupery

"You can't change the world. You can only change yourself."

Beatrice Wood

"One today is worth two tomorrows."

Benjamin Franklin

"Well begun is half done."

Proverb

Suggested Books:

A Weed Is a Flower: The Life of George Washington Carver, Aliki

First Grade Can Wait, Lorraine Aseltine

I Want to Be an Astronaut, Thomas Y. Crowell

Everyone Ready?, Franz Brandenberg

Timothy Turtle, Al Graham

Little Toot, Hardie Gramatky

Henry's Wild Morning, Margaret Greaves

Ben's Trumpet, Rachel Isadora

When I See My Dentist..., Susan Kuklin

When I See My Doctor..., Susan Kuklin

The Solo, Kathryn Lasky

Johnny's Eggs, Earlene Long

Andrew's Bath, David McPhail

Where's Jenna?, Margaret Miller

Dance, Tanya, Satomi Ichikawa

Tacky the Penguin, Helen Lester

Pig Pig Gets a Job, David McPhail

Ready, Alice?, Margo Mason

Be Ready at Eight, Peggy Parish

Alistair's Time Machine, Marilyn Sadler

Nobody Has Time for Me, Vladimir Skutina

Is Susan Here?, Janice May Urdry

Harry Gets Ready for School, Harriet Ziefert

(For a complete annotated listing of these books see the bibliography, page 96.)

Self-Reliance

DEFINITION:
To rely on one's own abilities, efforts or judgments.

MONDAY: The trait of the week is self-reliance. Self-reliance means to rely on one's own abilities, efforts or judgments. You can show self-reliance by always trying your best at school. Be sure to have the confidence to make your own decisions and stick with them in good times and bad. Discuss how you can use self-reliance today at school.

TUESDAY: The trait of the week is self-reliance. Self-reliance means to rely on one's own abilities, efforts or judgments. Don was working on his social studies homework. The assignment was to color a map of the United States. He was just starting, when he read one of the directions. It said to color the Great Lakes blue. Don checked his crayons and he did not have a blue crayon. Don wondered what to do. If he did not complete the assignment he would receive a bad grade. Suddenly he had an idea. "I know!" said Don "I'll color the Great Lakes purple. Purple is close to blue and I will still be able to complete my assignment." Discuss whether you think Don made a good decision by relying on his own judgment.

WEDNESDAY: The trait of the week is self-reliance. Self-reliance means to rely on one's own abilities, efforts or judgments. Cheryl was bored at recess. She asked the recess teachers what she could do. They suggested playing soccer or swinging on the swings. Cheryl didn't want to do that. What she really wanted to do was play hopscotch. She asked her friends what they were doing. "We're jumping rope. Why don't you join us?" Cheryl didn't want to jump rope, but she relied on her friend's advice and starting jumping rope. Cheryl didn't have a good time. When recess was over, she was disappointed that she had wasted all her free time. Discuss if you think Cheryl would have had a better time by being self-reliant, instead of relying on others.

THURSDAY: The trait of the week is self-reliance. Self-reliance means to rely on one's own abilities, efforts or judgments. Kenny's mother was called into work unexpectedly. "Kenny", she said. "I need to go to work early. Please look after you sister until I get home at 7:00." Kenny played games with his sister. Soon it was 5:00 and they were hungry. Kenny said, "We could wait for mother to get home in two hours. Or I have a better idea! Here is bread, peanut butter and jelly. I can make sandwiches." When Kenny's mom got home she was very proud of Kenny. "I knew I could rely on you Kenny." Discuss how Kenny used self-reliance to take care of his sister and himself.

FRIDAY: The trait of the week is self-reliance. Self-reliance means to rely on one's own abilities, efforts or judgments. Tim's dad was at a basketball game with his little brother. They would not be home until late. Tim was very upset. He needed to bring something to the Bake Sale at school tomorrow. By the time his father got home, it would be too late to go to the store. Tim couldn't bake anything because he was not allowed to use the oven. Then Tim had a great idea. He had construction paper and crayons. He could make some book marks to sell at the sale. He hoped his teacher would like them. The next day, Tim's teacher said, "I am so impressed by this clever idea Tim! I am sure everyone will want to buy a bookmark." Discuss how being self-reliant allowed Tim to make a neat idea for the Bake Sale.

Thoughts to Ponder:

"Every man must educate himself. His books and teachers are but helps; the work is his."

Daniel Webster

"You have to expect things of yourself before you can do them."

Michael Jordan

"If I am not for myself, who will be?"

Pirke Auoth

"Even if you are on the right track you'll get run over if you just sit there."

Will Rogers

"You cannot escape the responsibility of tomorrow by evading it today."

Abraham Lincoln

Suggested Books:

Donald Says Thumbs Down, Nancy Evans Cooney

The Strongest One of All, Mirra Ginsburg

Help, Laura Greene

Sara and the Door, Virginia Allen Jensen

I Can Do It By Myself, Lessie Jones Little and Eloise Greenfield

I Was So Mad, Mayer Mercer

The Little Engine That Could, Piper Watty

Can I Help?, Anne and Harlow Rockwell

Oliver, Amanda and Grandmother Pig, Jean Val Leeuwen

I Can Ride It!, Shigeo Watanabe

Where's My Daddy?, Shigeo Watanabe

I Can Build a House, Shigeo Watanabe

Someday, Sied Mitchell, Barbara Williams

The Hating Book, Charlotte Zolotow

(For a complete annotated listing of these books see the bibliography, page 80.)

Perseverance

DEFINITION:
To continue to do something in spite of difficulties.

MONDAY: The trait of the week is perseverance. Perseverance is to continue to do something in spite of difficulties. Many times at school you may be asked to learn difficult and challenging new ideas. A student who keeps trying, and does not give up will find a way to master these difficulties. Discuss how perseverance can help you be a better person at school or at home.

TUESDAY: The trait of the week is perseverance. Perseverance is to continue to do something in spite of difficulties. Judy was trying out for the school play. Every night she would practice memorizing her lines. Sometimes when she would recite her lines to her mother, she would forget everything. Judy kept trying. She studied on the bus and at lunch. She was determined not to give up. At the auditions Judy made a few small mistakes, but she got a part in the play! Judy was very excited. Discuss if you think Judy would have got the part in the play, if she had quit trying.

WEDNESDAY: The trait of the week is perseverance. Perseverance is to continue to do something in spite of difficulties. Diana was trying out for the basketball team. She thought all the other girls were faster than she was, and made better shots. Each night of tryouts she would come home discouraged. "I'm never going to make the team" she told her mother. "Don't give up!" Her mother encouraged her, "Just try your best." But on the last day of tryouts, Diana did not stay for practice. She thought she would not be picked, and gave up. Later Diana found out that every girl who went to all the tryout practices made the basketball team. Discuss how this story may have had a different ending if Diana had persevered and followed her mother's advice.

THURSDAY: The trait of the week is perseverance. Perseverance is to continue to do something in spite of difficulties. Tom was trying to build a model airplane his uncle had given him for his birthday. This was the first model Tom had build by himself. He read the directions over and over before he began. He worked slowly and carefully. Once he realized he had the wheels on backward and had to take everything apart and start all over. When he finished his model looked great. His dad told him, "You can really tell you worked hard on that Tom." Have you ever started a job that seemed very difficult? What might be some tips to help someone finish a difficult project?

FRIDAY: The trait of the week is perseverance. Perseverance is to continue to do something in spite of difficulties. Danny asked his parents if he could have a job of cutting two neighbor's yards all summer. His parents discussed with Danny the importance of doing a good job and sticking with it. Throughout the summer Danny had second thoughts about his job. Sometimes he had to miss playing with friends, or going to the pool to cut grass. Some days his shoulders hurt from pushing the lawn mower. Many times he wanted to quit, but he stuck with it. At the end of the summer he had money to put into his savings account and buy new roller blades. He felt very proud.

Thoughts to Ponder:

"Diligence is the mother of good luck."

French proverb

"Learning is not attained by chance, it must be sought for with ardor and attended to with diligence."

Abigal Adams

"You win one day, you lose the next day, you don't take it personally. You get up every day and go on."

Hillary Rodham Clinton

"Drop by drop fills the tub."

French proverb

"Small strokes fell great oaks."

Old proverb

Suggested Books:

D.W. Flips!, Marc Brown
See How They Grow: Kittens, Jane Burton and Angela Royston
The Waiting Day, Harriet Diller
Good As New, Barbara Douglass
Patience, What Is It?, Beverly Fiday
Once Around the Block, Kevin Henkes

Grandma Gets Grumpy, Anna Grossnickle Hines
Not Yet, Yvette, Mary Kettleman
Leo the Late Bloomer, Robert Kraus
Little Things, Anne Laurin
Is It Bedtime?, Dave Ross
Max's Breakfast, Rosemary Wells

(For a complete annotated listing of these books see the bibliography, page 81.)

Sportsmanship

DEFINITION:

Using fair play or sportsmanlike conduct.

MONDAY: The trait of the week is sportsmanship. Sportsmanship is using fair play or sportsmanlike conduct. You can show sportsmanship by remembering to keep complaints or bragging to yourself during any competition. Always use appropriate language, and do not name call or put others down during an event or game. Good sportsmanship can also be shown by congratulating the other team after the game or shaking hands with your opponent. Discuss how you can use sportsmanship today at school.

TUESDAY: The trait of the week is sportsmanship. Sportsmanship is using fair play or sportsmanlike conduct. Chad could hardly wait for the big soccer game. Finally the day of the game arrived. Chad scored the only goal in the game and his team won! Chad was so happy he wanted to jump around the field, but immediately after the game he lined up to shake the hands of the other team. To each player he said, "Good game!" Chad's mother was very happy that he had won. But after the game she said, "Chad I am happy you won, but I also like how you showed good sportsmanship by playing fair and then congratulating the other team. You made me very proud of you!" Discuss how you think Chad showed good sportsmanship.

WEDNESDAY: The trait of the week is sportsmanship. Sportsmanship is using fair play or sportsmanlike conduct. Destini and Khristian were each on a track team. On Saturday, Destini's team was scheduled to race against Khristian's team. When Khristian found out she told Destini, "You are going to lose, because I am much faster than you are!" Destini didn't say anything but she felt very bad about what Khristian had said. On Saturday both girls lined up to race. Destini wanted to beat Khristian and show her that she really was a fast runner. When Destini crossed the finish line first, she couldn't believe it! She ran over to Khristian and shouted, "Now we see who is the loser! I am the winner!" Khristian was very upset, but she just walked away. Discuss whether you think either girl showed sportsmanship.

THURSDAY: The trait of the week is sportsmanship. Sportsmanship is using fair play or sportsmanlike conduct. Paula and Erica both wanted to try out for the school play. Each girl wanted to try out for the lead part. After the girls auditioned, they waited for the director to make his decision. The director choose Paula to play the lead role. All of the girls clapped and cheered for Paula. When Erica hugged Paula she said, "I am so happy for you! Congratulations!" The director overheard Erica. He said, "That really shows good sportsmanship when you congratulate someone you were competing against." Good sportsmanship can be used outside of sports. Discuss how good sportsmanship was shown by the girls.

FRIDAY: The trait of the week is sportsmanship. Sportsmanship is using fair play or sportsmanlike conduct. Andrew and Ben were playing basketball after school. The game was tied and it was getting late. Andrew was trying to dribble when his foot got tangled up and he fell. Ben grabbed the loose ball and could have taken the ball and made a basket to win the game. Instead he let the ball roll away and bent over to offer Andrew his hand to help him up. "Hey!" Andrew said. "Why didn't you take the ball and score? Ben said, "It wouldn't have been the same with you hurting your ankle. I like to play ball, but I wouldn't want you to get hurt. We can always play again tomorrow." Discuss how using good sportsmanship builds good friendships.

Thoughts to Ponder:

"A cheerful loser is a winner."

Elbert Hubbard

"When the sun is shining I can do anything; no mountain is too high, no trouble too difficult to overcome."

Wilma Rudolph (Olympic track star)

"If you don't have confidence, you'll always find a way not to win."

Carl Lewis

"You may be on top of the heap—but remember you're still part of it."

Frances Rodman

"What we see depends mainly on what we look for."

John Lubbock

Suggested Books:

School Isn't Fair, Patricia Baehr

The Berenstain Bears Ready, Set, Go!, Stan and Jan Berenstain

Let's Talk About Being a Bad Sport, Joy Wilt Berry

Bet You Can't, Penny Dale

The Monkey and the Crocodile, Paul Galdone

It's Not Fair, Anita Harper

It's Not Fair!, Deborah Hautzig

Keep Your Old Hat, Anna Grossnickle Hines

Angelina and Alice, Katharine Holabird

Albert the Running Bear Gets the Jitters, Barbara Isenbery and Susan Wolf

Old Turtle's Soccer Team, Leonard Kessler

Playing Fair, Shelley Nielsen

Garden Partners, Diane Palisciano

That's Not Fair, Jane Sarnoff and Reynold Ruffins

You're a Good Sport, Charlie Brown, Charles M. Schultz

Mufaro's Beautiful Daughters, An African Tale, John Steptoe

Excuse Me, But It's My Turn, Karen Romano Young

The Quarreling Book, Charlotte Zolotow

(For a complete annotated listing of these books see the bibliography, page 90.)

Self-Discipline

DEFINITION:
To control one's emotions or actions.

MONDAY The trait of the week is self-discipline. Self-discipline means to control one's emotions or actions. You can show self-discipline by always thinking before you act. Try not to make hasty decisions that you will later regret. Having self-discipline is not easy, but it is a trait that will be noticed and appreciated by others. Discuss how you can use self-discipline today at school.

TUESDAY: The trait of the week is self-discipline. Self-discipline means to control one's emotions or actions. Chris went to watch her sister's basketball game. She could not find a seat by her parents, so she sat by herself. Throughout the game the woman sitting next to Chris complained loudly about Chris's sister. She called her "lazy" and "untalented". The lady wondered why the coach didn't put in another player to replace Chris's sister. Listening to these comments made Chris very angry. She wanted to speak out, but didn't. After the game Chris talked to her parents about it. Her mother said, "I am very glad you had control over your emotions. Thinking before you act really shows maturity." Discuss how the ending of this story may have changed if Chris had talked out.

WEDNESDAY: The trait of the week is self-discipline. Self-discipline means to control one's emotions or actions. Cory was playing soccer. His team was losing, and the other team was playing a very physical game. The opposing players were going after every lose ball and sometimes bumping into players on Cory's team. Cory was becoming angry that his team was getting beat. When he went to kick a ball, a player from the other team knocked him down. The referee blew his whistle and called a foul, but Cory did not listen. He got to his feet and started yelling and shoving the other player. Cory was then thrown out of the game. Discuss what Cory could have done to use self-discipline in this situation.

THURSDAY: The trait of the week is self-discipline. Self-discipline means to control one's emotions or actions. A new girl moved into Holly's class. Holly did not know why, but the new girl did not seem to like her. She teased her and called her names. Holly asked her to stop, but it just got worse. The new girl spread rumors that she was going to fight Holly. That day at recess the new girl called Holly a "chicken" and tried to get her to fight. Holly walked away and told the teacher. Discuss how Holly used self-discipline to stay out of trouble.

FRIDAY: The trait of the week is self-discipline. Self-discipline means to control one's emotions or actions. Zach wanted to make his Grandmother a special present for her birthday. He was going to paint a picture. But every time he started the picture, something went wrong. The paint spilled, or the picture didn't look exactly right. Zach's mother saw him wadding up a painting and throwing it out. He looked frustrated and angry. "Zach" his mother said, "Getting angry and losing your temper is not going to help your painting. Why not try take a break, or try working on something else, or ask for help before you lose your temper." Zach took his mother's advice, and finally he created a painting he was really proud of. Discuss some tips you have for controlling your emotions.

Thoughts to Ponder:

"Do not cut down the tree that gives you shade."

Arabian proverb

"Let your conscience by your guide."

Jiminy Cricket

"It is easier to talk than hold one's tongue."

Greek proverb

"Words fitly spoken are like apples of gold."

Old proverb

"Your opinion of others is apt to be their opinion of you."

B.C. Forbes

Suggested Books:

Donald Says Thumbs Down, Nancy Evans Cooney

The Strongest One of All, Mirra Ginsburg

Help, Laura Greene

Sara and the Door, Virginia Allen Jensen

I Can Do It By Myself, Lessie Jones Little and Eloise Greenfield

I Was So Mad, Mayer Mercer

The Little Engine That Could, Piper Watty

Can I Help?, Anne and Harlow Rockwell

Oliver, Amanda and Grandmother Pig, Jean Val Leeuwen

I Can Ride It!, Shigeo Watanabe

Where's My Daddy?, Shigeo Watanabe

I Can Build a House, Shigeo Watanabe

Someday, Sied Mitchell, Barbara Williams

The Hating Book, Charlotte Zolotow

(For a complete annotated listing of these books see the bibliography, page 80.)

Independence

> **DEFINITION:**
> The condition of being independent; freedom

MONDAY: The trait of the week is independence. Independence is the condition of being independent; freedom. As you grow older you will receive more independence at school and at home. You will be allowed to make more of your own choices and decisions. However, you will also need to learn that with independence there is responsibility. You will need to act responsibly for the actions you take. How can learning to handle independence, help you to become a responsible citizen?

TUESDAY: The trait of the week is independence. Independence is the condition of being independent; freedom. Josh's father had some shopping to do. Josh had some homework he needed to finish. Josh's father said, "Josh, I would let you stay home to work on your assignments, but I can't find a babysitter at this late notice." Josh talked to his father about staying home alone. They discussed that Josh was old enough to stay at home if he understood and obeyed the house rules. Josh's father finally agreed that he could stay by himself. While his father was gone, Josh followed all the rules they had discussed. When his father returned, he complimented Josh for getting his homework done and following all the rules. Discuss how Josh's father would have felt if Josh was not responsible.

WEDNESDAY: The trait of the week is independence. Independence is the condition of being independent; freedom. Jacob asked his mother for permission to ride his bike to the library after school. Jacob's mother said he could, but he must remember the conditions of this extra independence. He must still be on time for dinner, he was not to talk to strangers and he was not to go anywhere but the library. Jacob did not handle his freedom very well. He skipped going to the library and went to a friend's house. He arrived home late for dinner. When Jacob's mother found out, she was very disappointed in him. She told Jacob that she was taking away this extra independence until he could show that he was responsible enough to handle it. Discuss when is the age you believe a child should be given more independence. What signs would let you know if a child could handle any extra freedom?

THURSDAY: The trait of the week is independence. Independence is the condition of being independent; freedom. Felita was born in Cuba. She came to the United States when she was 13. She was amazed by the freedoms that were enjoyed by the American people. In school she wrote an essay about the freedom of speech and religion. She told her classmates to appreciate and be thankful for their independence. Discuss why the United States receives immigrants who wish to live in our country.

FRIDAY: The trait of the week is independence. Independence is the condition of being independent; freedom. Bridgett's mother always went to Bridgett's gymnastics class with her. Her mother did not sit quietly on the sidelines and watch. Instead she would constantly correct Bridgett and the other students, and interrupt the lesson. Bridgett was very upset by this behavior. Although she knew it might hurt her mother's feelings, one day after class she told her the truth. "Mother, " said Bridgett. "I am afraid I will never become an independent person if you are always there correcting me and making decisions for me. Please allow me some freedom, so that I can be responsible for my actions." Discuss if you think Bridgett's mother will allow her to become more independent.

Thoughts to Ponder:

"A person has to live with themselves, and they should see to it that they always have good company."

Charles Evans Hughes

"If, at the end, I have lost every friend on earth, I shall have one friend left and that friend shall be down inside me."

Abraham Lincoln

"There can be no real freedom without the freedom to fail."

Eric Hoffer

"No one is rich enough to do without a neighbor."

Danish proverb

"You may have to fight a battle more than once to win it."

Margaret Thatcher

Suggested Books:

My First Fourth of July Book, Harriet Hodgson

Pimm's Place, Beverly Keller

The Inside-Outside Book of Washington, D.C., Roxie Munro

The Rainbow Fish, Marcus Pfister

Ruby The Copycat, Peggy Rathmann

Eggbert, Tony Ross

The Little Engine That Saved The City, Dennis Smith

(For a complete annotated listing of these books see the bibliography, page 101.)

Neatness

DEFINITION:
Orderly, tidy and clean

MONDAY: The trait of the week is neatness. Neatness is to be orderly, tidy and clean. Being neat at school can be a great asset. If your papers are neat and your desk is clean, you will not need to worry about lost assignments. If you are organized you will know when assignments are due and will set a good example for classmates. Discuss how you can use neatness today at school.

TUESDAY: The trait of the week is neatness. Neatness is to be orderly, tidy and clean. Shamarr had a special folder for his school work. One side was labeled "Take Home" and one side was labeled "To Do". Some of the other students in class just stuffed their papers anywhere into their desks. Shamarr used his folder and was always careful where he put papers. He never lost papers or missed assignments because of his organization. Discuss if you have a system to be organized at school.

WEDNESDAY: The trait of the week is neatness. Neatness is to be orderly, tidy and clean. Travis was not very neat. At school, his desk and backpack were messy. His room at home was also not very tidy. His mother was always asking Travis to take responsibility for being neat, but Travis did not listen to her. On his birthday, Travis's Grandmother gave him a gift certificate to his favorite store. Travis tossed the gift certificate into his room. Later he could not find it and was angry. His mother would not help him look for it. She said,"I have told you many times about being more tidy, Travis." "That's not fair!" said Travis. Discuss who was responsible for finding the gift certificate, Travis or his mother?

THURSDAY: The trait of the week is neatness. Neatness is to be orderly, tidy and clean. Lakeisha always took pride in her appearance. Her school uniform always looked orderly and clean. One day the principal saw Lakeisha in the hallway. He said, "Thank you for taking an interest in your appearance! I appreciate how you neat you look every day." Those words made Lakeisha feel very good. Discuss how a messy appearance might give a bad impression to someone who meets you for the first time.

FRIDAY: The trait of the week is neatness. Neatness is to be orderly, tidy and clean. Jameesa was painting a project in Art class. The teacher asked the students to put on a painting shirt and to cover the tables with newspaper. Jameesa followed the teacher's directions. She worked carefully with the paint and made a beautiful painting. Some students did not follow directions, or were messy with the paint. They had paint on their school clothes and on the tables. The teacher complimented Jameesa by saying, "I like how neatly Jameesa has completed this project." Discuss why neatness is important in all subject areas.

Thoughts to Ponder:

"Behavior is a mirror, in which everyone shows his image."

Goethe

"Good order is the foundation of all things."

Edmund Burke

"Order marches with weighty and measured strides; disorder is always in a hurry."

Napoleon

"If each one sweeps before his own door, the whole street will be clean."

Yiddish proverb

"There is no shame in getting dirty, the blame is in staying that way."

Author unknown

Suggested Books:

The Berenstain Bears and the Messy Room, Stan and Jan Berenstain

Let's Talk About Being Messy, Joy Berry

Teach Me About Bathtime, Joy Berry

Messy, Barbara Bottner

Clean Your Room, Harvey Moon!, Pat Cummings

You Need a Bath, Mustard, Paul Dowling

Bert & Susie's Messy Tale, Jim Erskine

Swampy Alligator, Jack Gantos

It's Your Turn, Roger!, Susanna Gretz

Roger Loses His Marbles!, Susanna Gretz

Dirty Larry, Bobbie Hamsa

Eeps Creeps, It's My Room!, Martha Whitmore Hickman

The Woman Who Lived in Holland, Mildred Howelss

Stop Stop, Eddith Thacher Hurd

Tidy Titch, Pat Hutchins

The Pigrates Clean Up, Steven Kroll

To Bathe a Boa, C. Imbior Kudrna

Let's Give Kitty a Bath!, Steven Lindblom

Tidy Up, Trevor, Rob Lewis

Messy Bessy, Patricia and Fredrick McKissick

Messy Bessy's Closet, Patricia and Fredrick McKissick

Tidy Pig, Lucinda McQueen and Jeremy Guitar

Eleanora Mousie Makes a Mess, Ann Morris

Marianna May and Nursey, Tomie DePaola

When the Fly Flew In..., Lisa Westberg Peters

Day Care ABC, Tamara Phillips

The Tale of Mrs. Tittlemouse, Beatrix Potter

Nice and Clean, Anne and Harlow Rockwell

K is for Kiss Good Night: A Bedtime Alphabet, Jill Sardegna

The Seven Sloppy Days of Phineas Pig, Mitchell Sharmat

Spiffen, A Tale of a Tidy Pig, Mary Ada Swartz

Pigsty, Mark Teague

Oh, What a Mess, Hans Wilhelm

(For a complete annotated listing of these books see the bibliography, page 98.)

Resourcefulness

DEFINITION: Skillful and imaginative in finding ways of doing things or resolving difficulties.

MONDAY: The trait of the week is resourcefulness. Resourcefulness is to be skillful and imaginative in finding ways of doing things or resolving difficulties. No two people learn in exactly the same way. Therefore, you may need to be resourceful when learning new ideas or concepts at school. For example, if you are struggling to learn your multiplication facts you might try writing them down. Or say them aloud into a tape recorder and then play it back. Or make flashcards and study with a friend. Discuss different ways you can be resourceful at school today.

TUESDAY: The trait of the week is resourcefulness. Resourcefulness is to be skillful and imaginative in finding ways of doing things or resolving difficulties. Darnell's sister, Lindsee was playing with her Barbies. She kept telling her mother she wanted to buy the Barbie car for her dolls. Finally her mother told her there was not enough money for the expensive Barbie car. Lindsee began crying, and Darnell's mother looked upset too. Darnell went to his room. He took an empty shoe box and drew doors on it. Then he took his markers and added details. When he gave it to Lindsee she was thrilled! She put her Barbies in the "car". Darnell's mother told him, "Thank you for being so resourceful, you made your sister very happy." Discuss if you have ever made a neat toy for yourself instead of buying one.

WEDNESDAY: The trait of the week is resourcefulness. Resourcefulness is to be skillful and imaginative in finding ways of doing things or resolving difficulties. Reggie's teacher gave each student a small bag of items. She told the students their assignment was to create a story using each item in the bag, in the story. Reggie dumped out her bag. She had a seashell, a feather and a marble. "This is stupid, " she said, "I can't write a story about that." She put down her pencil and didn't write anything. All the other students went right to work. When it came time to share the stories, all the students had written wonderful, imaginative stories except Reggie. Discuss how you think Reggie felt after hearing her classmates stories.

THURSDAY: The trait of the week is resourcefulness. Resourcefulness is to be skillful and imaginative in finding ways of doing things or resolving difficulties. Ashley was in the library. She was trying to find books for the Science Fair. She had not found any and her mother was coming in one hour to pick her up. Then she had an idea. She used the computer to look up different, science related words. She was amazed when she found books on experiments, demonstrations and science fair tips. There were also videos and magazines. When her mother came to pick her up, Ashley had all the materials she needed. Being resourceful sometimes means trying different ways. How did Ashley not give up?

FRIDAY: The trait of the week is resourcefulness. Resourcefulness is to be skillful and imaginative in finding ways of doing things or resolving difficulties. Sammy and Janae were sitting at the same table. They did not get along. Neither one would cooperate and they were constantly tattling on one another. Finally their teacher had enough. She told them they must stay in at recess and find a way to resolve their differences. Sammy and Janae made lists of what they thought they needed to change. Then they rearranged their table and made "Do Not Disturb" signs for each other. When their teacher saw the imaginative ways they had created to resolve their differences she was very impressed. Discuss other resourceful ways that Sammy and Janae might use to end their conflict.

Thoughts to Ponder:

"To turn an obstacle to one's advantage is a great step towards victory."

French proverb

"If you learn to THINK BIG, nothing on earth will keep you from being successful."

Benjamin Carson

"When it is dark enough, you can see the stars."

Charles A. Beard

"Necessity is the mother of invention."

Proverb

"Be prepared."

Boy Scout Motto

Suggested Books:

The Bird, the Frog, and the Light, Avi
Everyone Ready?, Franz Brandenberg
Sam And The Tigers, Julius Lester
The Boy Who Held Back The Sea, Thomas Locke,
  retold by Lenny Hart
The Giving Tree, Shel Silverstein
Becky And The Bear, Dorothy Van Woerkam

(For a complete annotated listing of these books see the bibliography, page 101.)

Peacefulness

DEFINITION:
The state of being calm, tranquil and quiet.

MONDAY: The trait of the week is peacefulness. Peacefulness is the state of being calm, tranquil and quiet. You can show peacefulness at school by working quietly with classmates. At recess, remember to take turns and share. Discuss how you can use peacefulness today at school.

TUESDAY: The trait of the week is peacefulness. Peacefulness is the state of being calm, tranquil and quiet. Joseph was spending the night at his Grandmother and Grandfather's house. It was very cold out, so his Grandfather started a fire in the fireplace. His Grandmother made hot chocolate. They sat together listening to the wind blow outside and the crackle of the fire. His Grandmother began to sew. Joseph and his Grandfather read books. "You know Grandmother," Joseph said, "This is really peaceful." Discuss how how television or video games may have changed this peaceful evening.

WEDNESDAY: The trait of the week is peacefulness. Peacefulness is the state of being calm, tranquil and quiet. Carlo's class had indoor recess. Their teacher told them that they needed to find a quiet activity to do. Some students were drawing, some were playing cards and some students were reading. Carlo didn't want to do those things. He began talking loudly across the room to another boy. Then he took his pencils and was banging them on his desk like a drum. When his teacher checked in on the class, everyone was quiet but Carlo. Discuss some peaceful activities that Carlo could have chosen to do.

THURSDAY: The trait of the week is peacefulness. Peacefulness is the state of being calm, tranquil and quiet. Monique had a broken leg. She could not run around to play. Sitting inside was making her frustrated and irritable. One day her Aunt brought over a 1,000 piece puzzle. She took everything off the kitchen table and set out the puzzle pieces. She turned on some soft music. Monique and her Aunt began to work on the puzzle. It was very peaceful. When Monique looked at the clock she was shocked to see two hours had passed, and she hadn't thought once of her broken leg! Discuss if you have ever enjoyed a quiet activity by yourself or with a friend.

FRIDAY: The trait of the week is peacefulness. Peacefulness is the state of being calm, tranquil and quiet. Michael was going to a family reunion. His mother said he would meet his cousin, Dwayne. Michael was not looking forward to getting stuck all day with his cousin. However when he met Dwayne, Michael was pleased to find out they had many things in common. Both boys liked basketball and Legos. Dwayne had even brought a large Lego set with him. The boys spent all day building Legos. When he left, Michael told his mom, "I can't believe what a great time I had!" His mother said, "The grownups couldn't believe how peacefully you two played! I am very proud of you!" Discuss why some people are easier to get along with than others. Do you consider yourself a peaceful person?

Thoughts to Ponder:

"Always aim at complete harmony of thought, word and deed. Always aim at purifying your thoughts and everything will be well."

Mohandas K. Gandhi

"Before we set our hearts too much upon anything, let us examine how happy they are, who already possess it."

Francois de La Rochefoucould

"We hate some persons because we do not know them—and will not know them because we hate them."

Charles Caleb Cotton

"Much happiness is overlooked because it doesn't cost anything."

Author unknown

"It isn't your position that makes you joyful or unhappy. It is your disposition."

Author unknown

Suggested Books:

Who Belongs Here? An American Story, Margy
  Burns Knight
Watch Out for Chicken Feet in Your Soup,
  Tomie De Paola
Are You My Friend?, Janice Derby
Good Morning, Good Night, Ivan Gantschev
Just About Perfect, Kate Green
Pimm's Place, Beverly Keller
The Napping House, Audrey Wood

(For a complete annotated listing of these books see the bibliography, page 102.)

Cleanliness

DEFINITION:
Clean, free from dirt.

MONDAY: The trait of the week is cleanliness. Cleanliness means to be clean, free from dirt. you can show cleanliness at school by remembering to clean up after yourself. You should also remember to wash your hands and not to pick up any strange, or dirty items that you find at school or on the playground. Discuss how you can use cleanliness today at school.

TUESDAY: The trait of the week is cleanliness. Cleanliness means to be clean, free from dirt. Tyesha was eating lunch. When lunch was over, she remembered to clean up any wrappers or trash that were around the area where she was eating. As she walked to the trash can, she saw someone had left orange peels on the table. Even though it wasn't her trash, she picked it up and threw it out. Then Tyesha asked the custodian if she could use a sponge to help wash tables. Discuss how Tyesha was setting a good example at lunch by keeping the cafeteria clean.

WEDNESDAY: The trait of the week is cleanliness. Cleanliness means to be clean, free from dirt. Antonio was out on the playground during recess. He was sliding down the slide when he saw a cup from a fast food restaurant at the bottom of the slide. Antonio thought no one was looking so he picked up the dirty cup. He took the cup and started tearing it into little pieces. Then he threw the little pieces up in the air. Suddenly the teacher yelled, "Antonio! Come here!" When Antonio went over to the teacher she said, "We need to keep our playground clean. Look at the mess you made. Please clean up those little scraps." Antonio was very sullen. He said, "It wasn't my cup. Why should I have to clean it up?" Discuss if you think it should be Antonio's responsibility to clean up the mess.

THURSDAY: The trait of the week is cleanliness. Cleanliness means to be clean, free from dirt. Katie's school had a Clean Classroom Award. Every week the custodian would select the cleanest room. That winning room would receive a plaque. At the end of the year, the classroom with the most wins would receive a pizza party! Katie's class worked hard to keep the room clean. They would pick up paper, pencils and erasers from the floor. They stacked their chairs and made sure everything was neat. Discuss any routines your class uses to promote cleanliness.

FRIDAY: The trait of the week is cleanliness. Cleanliness means to be clean, free from dirt. Keith's class was studying the human body in Health class. Keith learned that germs can be spread in many ways. To prevent illness you should always wash your hands before eating. At school you may want to try an antibacterial hand lotion. At home remember to take baths and wash your clothes. As you grow up you will become more and more responsible for your own cleanliness. Take an interest in your personal hygiene so that you will be healthy and have a good feeling about yourself. Cleanliness is a sometimes a hard subject to discuss. How would you help someone who needs to be more aware of the cleanliness, without hurting their feelings or embarrassing them?

Thoughts to Ponder:

"Cleanliness is next to Godliness."

The Talmud

"A clean glove often hides a dirty hand."

English Proverb

"God looks at clean hands, not the full ones."

Publilius Syrus

"A hog ought not be blamed for being a hog, but a person ought."

Proverb

"A boy becomes a man when he walks around a puddle of water instead of through it."

Teacher overheard

Suggested Books:

The Berenstain Bears and the Messy Room, Stan and Jan Berenstain

Let's Talk About Being Messy, Joy Berry

Teach Me About Bathtime, Joy Berry

Messy, Barbara Bottner

Clean Your Room, Harvey Moon!, Pat Cummings

You Need a Bath, Mustard, Paul Dowling

Bert & Susie's Messy Tale, Jim Erskine

Swampy Alligator, Jack Gantos

It's Your Turn, Roger!, Susanna Gretz

Roger Loses His Marbles!, Susanna Gretz

Dirty Larry, Bobbie Hamsa

Eeps Creeps, It's My Room!, Martha Whitmore Hickman

The Woman Who Lived in Holland, Mildred Howelss

Stop Stop, Eddith Thacher Hurd

Tidy Titch, Pat Hutchins

The Pigrates Clean Up, Steven Kroll

To Bathe a Boa, C. Imbior Kudrna

Let's Give Kitty a Bath!, Steven Lindblom

Tidy Up, Trevor, Rob Lewis

Messy Bessy, Patricia and Fredrick McKissick

Messy Bessy's Closet, Patricia and Fredrick McKissick

Tidy Pig, Lucinda McQueen and Jeremy Guitar

Eleanora Mousie Makes a Mess, Ann Morris

Marianna May and Nursey, Tomie DePaola

When the Fly Flew In..., Lisa Westberg Peters

Day Care ABC, Tamara Phillips

The Tale of Mrs. Tittlemouse, Beatrix Potter

Nice and Clean, Anne and Harlow Rockwell

K is for Kiss Good Night: A Bedtime Alphabet, Jill Sardegna

The Seven Sloppy Days of Phineas Pig, Mitchell Sharmat

Spiffen, A Tale of a Tidy Pig, Mary Ada Swartz

Pigsty, Mark Teague

Oh, What a Mess, Hans Wilhelm

(For a complete annotated listing of these books see the bibliography, page 98.)

Courtesy

DEFINITION:
Politeness and consideration of others; good manners.

MONDAY: The trait of the week is courtesy. Courtesy is politeness and consideration of others; good manners. School can be a wonderful opportunity to demonstrate courtesy to teachers, classmates and other students. Remember to say "please" and "thank you". When you addressing an adult use "Sir" or "Ma'am" to show respect. Using courtesy will make you a standout student, and later in life a respected adult. Discuss how you can use courtesy today at school.

TUESDAY: The trait of the week is courtesy. Courtesy is politeness and consideration of others; good manners. Lee was nominated by his teacher for Student Of The Month. At a school assembly, Lee's teacher announced that Lee truly modeled courteous behavior. He was always polite and considerate of others. Lee never needed to be reminded to be respectful to adults. He would look at whoever might be speaking to him and answer "Yes, Sir" or "Yes, Ma'am". Lee's teacher asked him to come up in front of the assembled students. She gave him an award and shook his hand. Lee felt very proud. Discuss why is it, that it is easy to spot someone with good manners?

WEDNESDAY: The trait of the week is courtesy. Courtesy is politeness and consideration of others; good manners. Scotty and his sister were spending the night with his aunt and uncle. His aunt made them a snack before bedtime. Scotty told his aunt "Thank you, for the snack." His aunt told Scotty "Your welcome!" Then she said, "If you two have everything you need, I am going to go downstairs for awhile and do some laundry." Both Scotty and his sister said that was fine. When his aunt had left the room, Scotty said, "This is a crummy snack. I don't think our aunt is a very good cook. I wish we didn't have to stay here." Scotty did not know that his uncle was in the kitchen. When he saw his uncle, he knew his uncle had overhead him. Scotty felt really bad about his ill manners. Discuss why it is important to use good manners all the time, not just when you think someone is watching.

THURSDAY: The trait of the week is courtesy. Courtesy is politeness and consideration of others; good manners. Ellen had received many gifts during the holidays. Before she would open a gift, she would check the gift tag to see who it was from. Ellen would make sure she thanked that person for the present. After the holidays, Ellen wrote each person who gave her a present a short thank you note. Discuss if you think Ellen's politeness was appreciated by others.

FRIDAY: The trait of the week is courtesy. Courtesy is politeness and consideration of others; good manners. Jason's class went on a field trip to a farm. They listened carefully to their tour guide when she was talking. The class did not talk to each other while the tour guide was explaining parts of the farm. When anyone had a question for the tour guide, they remembered to raise their hand and wait to be called on. At the end of the tour, the class thanked the tour guide for the wonderful presentation. The tour guide complimented the group by saying, "This is one of the most well mannered groups I have ever had. You should be very proud of yourself." Discuss how people make good or bad impressions by the way they act.

Thoughts to Ponder:

"He who sows courtesy reaps friendship; and he who plants kindness gathers love."

Phillips Brooks

"Rudeness is the weak man's imitation of strength"

Eric Hoffer

"Teach us to give and not to count the cost."

Ignatius Loyola

"No joy can equal the joy of serving others."

Sai Baba

"Pleasant words are honey on the tongue and music to the ear."

Proverb

Suggested Books:

Saying I'm Sorry, Laura Alden

Eddycat Introduces Mannersville, Ada Barnett, Pam Manquen and Linda Papaport

Eddycat Teaches Telephone Skills, Ada Barnett, Pam Manquen and Linda Papaport

The Manners Book, June Behrens

The Berenstain Bears Forget Their Manners, Stan and Jan Berenstain

Let's Talk About Being Rude, Joy Wilt Berry

Perfect Pigs, An Introduction to Manners, Marc Brown and Stephen Krensky

Pass the Fritters, Critters, Cheryl Chapman

Dinner at Alberta's, Russell Hoban

The Muppet Guide to Magnificent Manners, James Howe

What Do You Say, Dear?, Sesyle Joslin

Saying Please, Jane Belk Moncure

Please...Thanks...I'm Sorry!, Jane Belk Moncure

Manners, Shelly Nielsen

Mind Your Manners, Peggy Parrish

"EXCUSE ME," Janet Riehecky

"I'M SORRY," Janet Riehecky

"AFTER YOU," Janet Riehecky

"THANK YOU," Janet Riehecky

Please and Thank You Book, Richard Scarry

Excuse Me! Certainly, Louis Slobodkin

Excuse Me, You're Standing in Front of the TV, Karen Romano Young

Excuse Me, May I Have an Extra Napkin?, Karen Romano Young

Please, May I Have a Pencil?, Karen Romano Young

Please Come to My Party, Karen Romano Young

Excuse Me, But It's My Turn, Karen Romano Young

(For a complete annotated listing of these books see the bibliography, page 91.)

Fairness

> **DEFINITION:** Not favoring one above another; just. following the right rules, honest.

MONDAY: The trait of the week is fairness. Fairness is not favoring one above another; just. Following the right rules and being honest are also fairness. You can show fairness at school by following the rules. Make an effort to get along with all students. Avoid taking sides with classmates just because they are your friends. Remember to treat others the way you would want to be treated. Discuss how you can use fairness today at school.

TUESDAY: The trait of the week is fairness. Fairness is not favoring one above another; just. Following the right rules and being honest are also fairness. During gym class, Rodney was picked by his teacher to be the referee of the kickball game. Most of Rodney's friends were on Team One. As referee, Rodney had to make some tough calls against his friends. Team One ended up losing the game. Rodney heard some of his friends whispering complaints at the end of the game. However, Rodney's teacher said, "I think we had an excellent referee today. He followed the rules and did not favor one side. Thanks for being fair Rodney." Discuss if you think it was fair for some of Rodney's friends to expect special treatment from him.

WEDNESDAY: The trait of the week is fairness. Fairness is not favoring one above another; just. Following the right rules and being honest are also fairness. Cassie's class was reviewing subtraction problems. The teacher asked two students to go to the chalkboard. Then she would call out a subtraction problem. Each student would race to get the right answer. On Cassie's first turn the problem was 20–10. Cassie wrote 9 and was incorrect. She said, "That's not fair! I wasn't ready." Cassie's second problem was 30–2. Cassie wrote 25 and was wrong. Then she said, "That's not fair! I'm getting all the hard problems." Discuss if you think Cassie's math problems were fair.

THURSDAY: The trait of the week is fairness. Fairness is not favoring one above another; just. Following the right rules and being honest are also fairness. Tony went to a babysitter after school until his dad got home from work. The babysitter, Mrs. Jones, relied on Tony to help with some of the younger children she watched. She asked Tony to pass out cookies for a snack. There were twelve cookies and three children, plus Tony to get the snack. Some of the kids were trying to beg for more cookies, but Tony gave each person three. Discuss when someone isn't fair, how does it make you feel?

FRIDAY: The trait of the week is fairness. Fairness is not favoring one above another; just. Following the right rules and being honest are also fairness. Sheena went to a carnival. She loved to ride the rides, but standing in line for a ride was frustrating. Sheena was waiting on her favorite ride. The woman in front had a young child with her. Without warning the child ran out of the line. The woman ran after her. When she came back with her child, she went to the end of the line. Sheena called to her, "Excuse me! You can have your place back in line. You were here before I was." The woman was very impressed by Sheena's behavior. Discuss if you had been Sheena, would you have given the same offer to a stranger?

Thoughts to Ponder:

"Injustice anywhere is a threat to justice everywhere."

Martin Luther King Jr.

"Do what you can, with what you have, where you are."

Theodore Roosevelt

"Every path has its puddle."

Anonymous

"What we see depends mainly on what we look for."

John Lubbock

"All men are equal; it is not birth but virtue alone, that makes the difference."

Voltaire

Suggested Books:

School Isn't Fair, Patricia Baehr

The Berenstain Bears Ready, Set, Go!, Stan and Jan Berenstain

Let's Talk About Being a Bad Sport, Joy Wilt Berry

Bet You Can't, Penny Dale

The Monkey and the Crocodile, Paul Galdone

It's Not Fair, Anita Harper

It's Not Fair!, Deborah Hautzig

Keep Your Old Hat, Anna Grossnickle Hines

Angelina and Alice, Katharine Holabird

Albert the Running Bear Gets the Jitters, Barbara Isenbery and Susan Wolf

Old Turtle's Soccer Team, Leonard Kessler

Playing Fair, Shelley Nielsen

Garden Partners, Diane Palisciano

That's Not Fair, Jane Sarnoff and Reynold Ruffins

You're a Good Sport, Charlie Brown, Charles M. Schultz

Mufaro's Beautiful Daughters, An African Tale, John Steptoe

Excuse Me, But It's My Turn, Karen Romano Young

The Quarreling Book, Charlotte Zolotow

(For a complete annotated listing of these books see the bibliography, page 90.)

Confidence

DEFINITION:
Faith in oneself; self-reliance.

MONDAY: The trait of the week is confidence. Confidence means to have faith in oneself; self-reliance. A good student must have confidence in their abilities. Having faith in yourself will allow you to try new things and challenge yourself. It is always easier not to try something, than to actually do it. Dare yourself to be the best! Discuss different ways you can show confidence at school today.

TUESDAY: The trait of the week is confidence. Confidence means to have faith in oneself; self-reliance. Nathan was on a Trivia Quiz Team at school. His team would compete against other teams at school by answering a variety of questions. Teams earned points for correct answers. Then the teams with the most points would move on to play other schools. Nathan's team was down to the last question. If they answered correctly, they would win. If they missed it, they would be eliminated. Nathan thought he know the answer, but he was still nervous. Finally Nathan trusted his instinct and answered the question. Nathan was correct! Discuss if having confidence means you will never be nervous or unsure.

WEDNESDAY: The trait of the week is confidence. Confidence means to have faith in oneself; self-reliance. Ann was on a basketball team. Every night the coach told the team to practice their foul shots. Ann never practiced. She knew she was a good player and did not need to practice shots. At the end of a game, Ann was getting ready to shoot free throws. Ann missed both shots and was shocked. Sometimes you can be overconfident. How did overconfidence hinder Ann's performance?

THURSDAY: The trait of the week is confidence. Confidence means to have faith in oneself; self-reliance. Taylor had a test in math class. He had studied the night before. That morning, he had reviewed some more with his mom. As he was leaving the house, his mother told him, "I know you can do this Taylor. Just relax and do your best." As Taylor looked at his test, he remembered his mother's words. He felt confident when he started the test. Discuss how you think Taylor will do on the test.

FRIDAY: The trait of the week is confidence. Confidence means to have faith in oneself; self-reliance. Linda was working on the school newspaper. So far she had only done small odd jobs and never written an actual article. This week Mrs. Zorron asked Linda to write an article on the girl's volleyball team. Linda was very excited, but very nervous about this extra responsibility. She told Mrs. Zorron she didn't know if she could do it. Mrs. Zorron told her to have confidence in her abilities. Linda broke the article down into small steps. She went to a volleyball game, talked to the players and coach then wrote her article. When Mrs. Zorron read Linda's article she was very pleased. "Linda, I knew you would do a great job!" If you do not try new things, you will never know how good a job you might have done. Discuss, why is it difficult to try new things?

Thoughts to Ponder:

"You can't climb the ladder of success with cold feet."

Author unknown

"No one can make you feel inferior without your consent."

Eleanor Roosevelt

"We have nothing to fear but fear itself."

Franklin D. Roosevelt

"You can only find out by trying."

Greek proverb

"They conquer who believe they can."

Latin proverb

Suggested Books:

Donald Says Thumbs Down, Nancy Evans Cooney

The Strongest One of All, Mirra Ginsburg

Help, Laura Greene

Sara and the Door, Virginia Allen Jensen

I Can Do It By Myself, Lessie Jones Little and Eloise Greenfield

I Was So Mad, Mayer Mercer

The Little Engine That Could, Piper Watty

Can I Help?, Anne and Harlow Rockwell

Oliver, Amanda and Grandmother Pig, Jean Val Leeuwen

I Can Ride It!, Shigeo Watanabe

Where's My Daddy?, Shigeo Watanabe

I Can Build a House, Shigeo Watanabe

Someday, Sied Mitchell, Barbara Williams

The Hating Book, Charlotte Zolotow

(For a complete annotated listing of these books see the bibliography, page 80.)

Bibliography

PUNCTUALITY AND PROMPTNESS

Adoff, Arnold. *In For Winter, Out for Spring*. Harcourt Brace Jovanovich. New York 1991.
    Summary: This is a wonderful collection of rhymes as a little girl celebrates the seasons.

Allen, Jeffery, illustrated by James Marshall. *Mary Alice, Operator Number 9,* Little Brown and
    Company. Boston and Torono. 1975.
    Summary: When an efficient duck, who gives the time over the telephone, gets sick, other
    animals who think her job is easy, try to take her place.

Berenstain, Stan and Jan. *The Berenstain Bears and Too Much Pressure*. Random House. New York. 1992.
    Summary: Members of the Bear family commit themselves to so many time-consuming
    activites that the resulting stress brings on a crisis and makes them admit that there are only so
    many hours in the day.

Blundell, Tony, *Joe on Sunday*. Dian Books for Young Readers. New York. 1987
    Summary: Every day Joe seems to be some different animal as he behaves from dawn to dusk
    like a pig, a lion, a mouse, a monkey, a monster, and a king, depending on how he feels.

Boyd, Selma and Pauline, illustrated by Patience Brewster. *I Met a Polar Bear*. Lothrop, Lee and
    Shepard Books. New York, 1983.
    Summary: A little boy is late for school because he meets animals along the way that need his help.

Burningham, John. *Time to Get Out of the Bath, Shirley*. Thomas Y. Crowell Company. New York. 1978.
    Summary: During her bath Shirley is off on a series of imaginative adventures about which her
    mother has no idea.

Carle, Eric. *The Grouchy Ladybug*. Harper Collins Publishers. 1977.
    Summary: A grouchy ladybug who is looking for a fight challenges everyone she meets regard-
    less of their size or strength. Small clocks indicate the time of day on each page. There is also
    information about ladybugs.

Carle, Eric. *Today is Monday*. Philomel Books. New York. 1993.
    Summary: Each day of the week brings a new food, until on Sunday all the world's children can
    come and eat it.

Carlstrom, Nancy White, illustrated by Bruce Degen. *It's About Time, Jesse Bear*. Macmillan
    Publishing Company. New York. 1990.
    Summary: From early morning to bedtime, rhymes present the activities of Jesse Bear as he
    dresses, plays and gets ready for bed.

Clarke, Ginette Lamont and Florence Stevens, illustrations by Odile Ouellet. *What if the Bus Doesn't Come?* Tundra Books of Northern New York. Plattsburgh. New York. 1990.
Summary: Mark and Melanie worry on the first day of school that the bus won't come on time. They keep packing food, toys and supplies until the bus arrives and Mother has to take all they have packed back home.

Fox, Mem, illustrated by Jane Dyer. *Time for Bed*. Gulliver Books. Harcourt Brace & Company. San Diego. 1993.
Summary: This book is enriched by beautiful water colors that show parents putting their babies to bed as darkness falls.

Galbraith, Kathy Osebold, illustrated by Irene Trivas. *Waiting for Jennifer*. Margaret K. McElderry Books. New York. 1990.
Summary: Nan and Thea wait for their mother's baby to be born. Nan wants to name it Jennifer because she already knows how to spell that name.

Gerstein, Mordicai. *The Sun's Day*. Harper and Row, Publishers. New York. 1989.
Summary: Beautiful illustrations show activities as the sun sweeps across the sky on its daily journey.

Hutchins, Pat. *Clocks and More Clocks*. Macmillian Publishing Company. New York. Reissued in 1994, originally published in 1970.
Summary: Mr. Higgins can't decide why his clocks tell different times throughout his house, until the clockmaker comes and carries his watch from floor to floor and room to room.

Janovitz, Marily. *Is It Time?* North-South Books. New York. 1994.
Summary: Little wolf goes from tub to bed, in this easy to read story that is told in rhyme.

Krensky, Stephen, illustrated by Maryann Cocca-Leffler. *Big Time Bears*. Little, Brown and Company. Boston 1989.
Summary: Each unit of time, from a second to a century, is explained by the bear family.

McMillan, Bruce. *Time To ...* Lothrop, Lee and Shephard Books. New York. 1989.
Summary: This book shows Harriet and her activities at each hour of the day.

Oppenheim, Shulamith Levey, illustrated by Lillian Hoban. *Waiting for Noah*. Harper & Row, Publishers. New York, 1990.
Summary: Noah enjoys his grandmother telling him how she waited for news on the day he was born.

Park, W.B. *Bakery Business*. Little, Brown and Company. Boston. 1983.
Summary: Billy Bunny has been sick for a long time. A bear and three chickens have many troubles getting his birthday cake delivered on time. They finally get there...right on time!!

Quackenbush, Robert. *Henry's Important Date*. Parent's Magazine Press. New York. 1981.
Summary: Henry is delayed in getting to his friend Clara's birthday party through no fault on his part.

Rockwell, Anne. *Bear Child's Book of Hours*. Thomas Y. Crowell. New York. 1987.
Summary: As the hours pass Bear Child moves through his day. Each activity shows the time on the face of the clock.

Singer, Marilyn, illustrated by Frane Lessac. *Nine O'Clock Lullaby*. Harper and Collins Publishers. New York. 1991.
Summary: This is a beautiful book that shows time zones around the world.

Steinmetz, Leon. *Clock in the Woods*. Harper & Row, Publishers. New York. 1979.
Summary: The animals in the forest buy watches and clocks from the greedy porcupine only to find that the sun is more reliable.

Weiss, Nicki, *Waiting*. Greenwillow Books. New York. 1981.
Summary: A little girl waiting for her mother senses many things she thinks signal her mother's return.

LOYALTY/PATRIOTISM

Brenner, Martha, illustrated by Donald Cook. *Abe Lincoln's Hat*. Random House. New York. 1994.
Summary: This book tells the life of Lincoln from the time he was a young lawyer. It has amusing illustrations and photos at the end.

Buntin, Eve, illustrated by Donald Carrick. *Wednesday's Surprise*. Clarion Books. New York. 1989.
Summary: Everyone thinks Grandmother is helping the child with her homework, until they have a wonderful surprise when Grandmother learns to read.

Corwin, Judith Hoffman, Patriotic Fun. Julian Messner. New York. 1985.
Summary: This is an activity book of crafts and designs to be used on various patriotic holidays.

Curle, Jock, illustrated by Bernadette Watts. *Four Good Friends*. North-South Books. New York. 1987.
Summary: Maria, the woodcutter's wife, befriends four hungry animals from the forest. Her rude husband, Simon, has bad manners which land him in jail. The animals repay Maria's kindness and teach Simon the value of loyal friendship.

Fisher, Aileen, illustrated by Lydia Halvorson. *My First President's Day Book*. Children's Press. Chicago. 1987.
Summary: This book tells of important events in the lives of George Washington and Abraham Lincoln.

Green, Norman, illustrated by Eric Carle. *The Hole in the Dike*. Thomas Y Crowell Company. New York. 1974.
Summary: The old Dutch story retold about the the little boy who saved his country from the sea.

Hodgson, Harriet, *My First Fourth of July Book*. Children's Press. Chicago. 1987.
Summary: Traditional celebrations of our nation's birthday are told in rhymes.

Kellog, Steven. *Best Friends*. Dial Books for Young Readers. New York. 1986.
Summary: Kathy feels betrayed when her best friend spends the summer away and has a good time, while Kathy is at home missing her.

Munro, Roxie. *The Inside-Outside Book of Washington, D.C.* E. P Dutton, New York. 1987.
Summary: Beautiful views of the inside and outside of many of the historic buildings in our nation's capital.

De Paola, Tomie. *Legend of the Bluebonnet*. Putnam. New York. 1993.
Summary: A yound Comanche girl proves her loyalty by giving the only thing she has to save the people. Where the ashes of her sacrificed doll touch the ground, bluebonnets grow.

Say, Allen. *Grandfather's Journey*. Houghton Mifflin Company. Boston. 1993.
Summary: A Japanese-American man recounts his grandfathers journey to America which he later also undertakes. Both experience love for both countries.

Schaffer, Libor, illustrated by Agnes Mathieu. *Arthur Sets Sails*. North-South Books. New York. 1987.
Summary: Arthur, the aardvark, wants an adventure so he sails away to Rosy Pig Island. It doesn't take long for him to realize that home is best.

CONFIDENCE/SELF-RELIANCE/SELF-CONTROL

Cooney, Nancy Evans, illustrated by Maxie Chambliss. *Donald Says Thumbs Down*. G.P. Putname's Sons. New York 1987.
Summary: Donald does all he can to break himself of the habit of sucking his thumb.

Ginsburg, Mirra, illustrated by Jose Aruego & Ariane Dewey. *The Strongest One of All*. Greenwillow Books. New York. 1977.
Summary: The lamb asks the ice, sun, cloud, rain, earth and grass who is the strongest one of all and reaches a surprising conclusion.

Greene, Laura, illustrated by Gretchen Mayo. *Help*. Human Scinces Press. New York. 1981.
Summary: This is an informational book about when we need to give and when we need to get help.

Jensen, Virginia Allen, illustrated by Ann Strugnell. *Sara and the Door*. Addison-Wesley, Reading. MA. 1977.
Summary: While trying to free herself from the front door. Sara learns about buttons.

Little, Lessie Jones and Eloise Greenfield, illustrated by Carole Byard. *I Can Do It By Myself*. Thomas Y. Crowell Company. New York. 1978.
Summary: Donny is determined to buy his mother's birthday present all by himself. He meets a scary challenge on the way home.

Mayer, Mercer. *I Was So Mad*. A Golden Book. New York. 1983.
Summary: Everything the little creature wants to do no one will allow. He decides to run away. When his mother says that he could, he used his self-control to wait until tomorrow to see if he was still so angry.

Piper, Watty, illustrated by Ruth Sanderson. *The Little Engine That Could*. Platt & Much, Publishers. New York. 1989.
Summary: The classic story retold, of the little engine that could, because he thought he could. This is a beautifully illustrated version.

Rockwell, Anne and Harlow. *Can I Help?* Macmillan Publishing Company. New York. 1982.
Summary: A little girl is happy to be growing in self-reliance as she helps others.

Val Leeuwen, Jean, illustrated by Ann Schweninger. *Oliver, Amanda and Grandmother Pig*. Dial Books for Young Readers. New York. 1987.
Summary: Grandmother's visit gives Amanda and Oliver a chance to show their good character traits.

Watanabe, Shigeo, illustrated by Vasuo Ohtomo. *I Can Ride It!* Philomel Books. New York. 1979.
Summary: Not content to ride his tricycle or two-wheeler, a little bear attempts more difficult feats.

Watanabe, Shigeo, illustrated by Vasuo Ohtomo. *Where's My Daddy?* Philmel Books. New York. 1979.
Summary: A little bear keeps searching for his daddy until he finds him. (This is an I can do it all by myself book).

Watanabe, Shigeo, illustrated by Vasuo Ohtomo. *I Can Build A House*. Philmel Books. New York. 1982.
Summary: Bear trusts himself to build a house.

Williams, Barbara, illustrated by Kay Chorao. *Someday, Said Michell*. E.P. Dutton & Company, Inc. New York. 1976.
Summary: As Mitchell plans how he will help his mother when he grows up, she tells how he can help now while he is still little.

Zolotow, Charlotte, illustrated by Ben Shecter. *The Hating Book*. Harper & Row, Publishers. New York. 1969.
Summary: A little girl has an argument with her friend. She thinks she hates her until she finds out how much she misses her. She used self-control to apologize.

PATIENCE/PERSEVERANCE

Brown, Marc. *D. W. Flips!* Joy Street Books, Little, Brown, and Company.
Summary: D. W. must persevere to learn to do flips.

Burton, Jane, photographer, written and edited by Angela Royston. *See How They Grow: Kittens*. Lodestar Books. Dutton. New York. 1991.
Summary: Photographs and text show the development of a kitten from birth to two weeks old.

Diller, Harriet, illustrated by Chi Chung. *The Waiting Day*. Green Tiger Press. Published by Simon and Schuster. New York. 1994.
Summary: A beggar teaches a busy ferryman an important lesson about the right way to use his time.

Douglass, Barbara, illustrated by Patience Brewster. *Good As New*. Lathrop, Lee and Shepard Books. New York. 1982.
Summary: When Grady's young cousin ruins his teddy bear, he patiently waits for grandpa to repair it.

Fiday, Beverly, illustrated by Christina Rigo. *Patience, What Is it?* The Child's World. Elgin, Illinois. 1986.
Summary: This book shows times when we must use patience: finishing a jigsaw puzzle, waiting for our birthdays, and learning how to tie shoes.

Henkes, Kevin, illustrated by Victoria Chess. *Once Around the Block*. Greenwillow Books. New York. 1987.
Summary: Annie has nothing to do while she waits for her father to come home. Her mother tells her to walk once around the block. She finds kind neighbors, and her father waiting for her when she returns.

Hines, Anna Grossnickle. *Grandma Gets Grumpy*. Clarion Books. New York. 1988
Summary: Five cousins spending the night with grandma find there is a limit to her patience.

Kettleman, Mary, illustrated by Irene Trivas. *Not Yet, Yvette*. Albert Whitman & Sons. Morton Grove, Illinois. 1992.
Summary: Yvette and her father plan a surprise birhtday party for her mother.

Kraus, Robert, illustrated by Jose Aurego. *Leo the Late Bloomer*. Windmill Books. New York. 1971.
Summary: Leo's parents must wait for him to develop at his own right time.

Laurin, Anne, illustrated by Ruth Sanderson. *Little Things*. Atheneum. New York. 1978.
Summary: Little things don't bother Mr. B., but when his wife keeps knitting a blanket instead of doing her work, and makes it so big he can't find her...he finally loses his patience.

Ross, Dave. *Is It Bedtime?* William Morrow and Company, Inc. New York. 1987.
Summary: Papa must have a lot of patience when getting Perky Puppy to bed.

Wells, Rosemary, *Max's Breakfast*. Dial Books for Young Readers. New York.
Summary: This east to read story tells of Max having to finish his eggs before he could have strawberries.

RESPONSIBILITY/DEPENDABILITY

Allard, Henry, *Miss Nelson Has A Field Day*. Houghton-Mifflin. Boston. 1985.
Summary: Miss Viola Swamp is back at Horace B. Smedley School to shape up the football team so they can win at least one game.

Bulla, Robert Clyde. *Shoeshine Girl*. Thomas Y. Crowell. New York. 1975.
Summary: Sarah takes a job at a shoeshine stand thinking she will earn money. She learns much more than just how to shine shoes and earn money.

Burton, Virginia Lee. *Mike Mulligan and His Steam Shovel*. Houghton-Mifflin Company. Boston. 1928. 1967.
Summary: Mike Mulligan's steam shovel is too old to compete with newer technology, the people of Poppersville find a way to keep the two faithful workers useful.

Galdone, Paul. *The Little Red Hen*. Clarion. New York. 1973.
Summary: The little red hen finds she must rely on her own efforts and abilities when all of her lazy friends refuse to help her.

Pemberton, N. And J. Riehecky, illustrated by I. Holhag and L. Jacobson. *Responsibility: What Is It?* Children's Press. Chicago. 1988.
Summary: This book suggests ways to show responsibility, such as remembering to feed kitty, eating one's peas, wearing boots in the rain.

Dr. Seuss. *Horton Hears a Who!* Random House. New York. 1954.
Summary: Horton, the faithful elephant, protects and defends the whos who live in a speck of dust.

Sharmat, Marjorie Weinman, illustrated by Victoria Chess. *Taking Care of Melvin*. Holiday House. New York. 1980.
Summary: Melvin is so busy taking care of everyone else that he neglects to take care of himself until he becomes ill. He and his friends learn some important lessons.

Smith, Dennis, illustrated by Joanne Maffia. *The Little Engine That Saved The City*. Doubleday. New York. 1990.
Summary: Reliable fire engine Number Four, retired in favor of new equipment, saves the day when the biggest fire the city has ever seen gets out of control.

Sommers, Tish, illustrated by Maggie Swanson. *A Bird's Best Friend*. A Sesame Street/Golden Press Book. 1986.
Summary: Big bird is thrilled when he is given a puppy by Granny Bird until he learns how much care a puppy must be given.

Tresselt, Alvin, illustrated by Henri Sorensen. *The Gift of the Tree*. Lathrop, Lee, and Shepard Books. New York. 1972, 1992.

Summary: This beautiful book traces the life cycle of an oak tree and describes the animals that depend on it for shelter and food.

Winthrop, Elizabeth, illustrated by Denise Saldutti. *I Think He Likes Me*. Harper & Row, Publishers. New York. 1980.

Summary: A little girl proves to her parents that she can be trusted with her new baby brother.

RESPECT/TOLERANCE/GOODWILL

Carlstrom, Nancy White, illustrated by Lisa Desimini. *Fish and Flamingo*. Little, Brown, and Company. Boston. 1993.

Summary: Two unlikely friends, Fish and Flamingo, spend their time together, and tell stories about their different lives. The illustrations are vivid and wonderful.

Cherry, Lynne. *Great Kapok Tree*. Harcourt-Brace Javonovich. San Diego, 1990.

Summary: The many animals that live in the kapok tree in the rainforest of Brazil try to convince the man with an ax to spare their home.

De Paloa, Tomie. **Watch Out for Chicken Feet in Your Soup**. Prentice Hall, Englewood Cliffs. NJ. 1975.

Summary: A young boy gains a new appreciation for his Italian grandmother when he sees her through the eyes of his friends.

Derby, Janice, illustrated by Joy Dunn Keenan. *Are You My Friend?* Herald Press. Scottdale, PA, 1993.

Summary: A child meets many people who are different, but who can still be friends.

Fiday, Veberly and Deborah Crowdy, illustrated by Kathryn Hutton. *Respect*. The Child's World. Elgin, Illinois. 1978.

Summary: Shows ways children show respect.

Gantschev, Ivan. *Good Morning, Good Night*. Picture Book Studio. Saxonville, MA. 1991.

Summary: Tells how the bragging sun and the quiet moon come to be friends and to respect and value their differences.

Green, Kate, illustrated by Steve Mark. *Just About Perfect*. The Child's Word. Makato. MN. 1993.

Summary: T-bone, the dinosaur, is basically happy, but she thinks of ways to change those around her to make life perfect.

McNutly, Faith, illustrated by Bob Marshall. *The Lady and the Spider*. Harper & Row, Publishers. New York. 1986.

Summary: A spider who lives in a head of lettuce is allowed to live when a lady respects its right to live.

Massie, Diane Redfield. *Cocoon*. Thomas Y. Crowell. New York. 1983.

Summary: This beautiful wordless book shows the respect a man gives a cocoon that produces a butterfly.

Pryor, Bonnie, illustrated by Maryjane Begin. *The Porcupine Mouse*. Morrow Junior Books. New York. 1988.

Summary: Two brothers set out on their own and find it hard to agree until they learn to respect each other's gifts and talents.

Wildsmith, Brian. *Python's Party*. Franklin Watts, Inc. New York. 1975.
Summary: Python is hungry, and the animals are wary when he invites them to a party to show his goodwill. Elephant saves the day.

KINDNESS/CONSIDERATION

Baker, Jeannie. *Home in the Sky*. Greenwillow Books. New York. 1984.
Summary: A pigeon with a kindly owner and a home on the roof of a building meets a boy who wants to keep him.

Baum, Louis, illustrated by Susan Varley. *After Dark*. The Overlook Press. Woodstock, New York. 1991.
Summary: When mother has to work late, her daughter waits up even though she is suppose to be asleep.

Carey, Mary, illustrated by Joe Giordano. *The Owl Who Loved Sunshine*. Golden Press. New York. 1977.
Summary: Leander, the owl, learned to love the sunshine in the meadow and to watch all of the day animals play. He was shunned as an improper owl. He was able to prove himself a kind friend when he fought with the weasel.

Christain, Mary Blount, illustrated by S. D. Schindler. *Penrod's Party*. Macmillan Publishers. New York. 1990.
Summary: This is an easy to read book of four stories telling how Griswald Bear and Penrod Porcupine are kind and considerate of each other.

Cosgrove, Stephen, illustrated by Wendy Edelson. *T. J. Flopp*. Multnomah Press. Portland, OR. 1989.
Summary: T. J. Flopp wants to be known as a fearsome hunter and trapper, but when he catches Felicia Fuzzybottom he finds that he has a considerate side to his nature.

Grifalconi, Ann. *Osa's Pride*. Little, Brown and Company. Boston, Toronto. London. 1990.
Summary: Osa's grandmother tells her a tale about the sin of pride and helps Osa gain a better perspective on what things are important.

Keats, Ezra Jack. *Jennie's Hat*. Harper Collins. New York. 1966.
Summary: Jennie is disappointed in the hat her aunt sent until her bird friends solve her problem.

Moncure, Jane Belk, illustrated by Helen Endres. *Caring: What Is It?* Child's World Press. Elgin, Illinois. 1980.
Summary: Presents ways a child can show caring behavior.

Neilsen, Shelly, illustrated by Virginia Kylbery. *Caring*. Abdo and Daughters. Minneapolis. 1992.
Summary: Poems show children being thoughtful and kind.

Testi, Deborah, illustrated by Kevin Klein. *They're Only Words*. Oceana Educational Communications. Dobbs Ferry. NY. 1990.
Summary: This is one of the Aware Bears books, that tells how words can hurt as badly as injuries.

Wildsmith, Brian. *The Lazy Bear*. Franklin Watts, Inc. New York. 1973.
Summary: A bear finds a woodcutter's wagon, but must learn a lesson in consideration when he makes his friends push him up the hill in return for a ride down.

CITIZENSHIP/OBEDIENCE

Arnold, Caroline, photographs by Carole Bertol. *Who Keeps Us Safe?* Franklin Watts. New York. 1982.
Summary: With photographs and easy to read text this book tells how police officers, fire fighters, and emergency people work to keep us safe.

Brenner, Barbara. *Wagon Wheels.* Harper and Row. New York. 1990.
Summary: Soon after the Civil War, an African-American family travels to Kansas to get free land promised in the Homestead Act.

Boggell, Phyliss and Jim Laster, illustrated by Stephanie McFetridge Britt. *Safe Sally Seatbelt and the Magic Click.* Children's Press. Chicago. 1974.
Summary: Abigail learns the importance of using her seat belt.

Hall, Donald. *The Ox-Cart Man.*
Summary: This beautiful book shows daily life in the changing seasons of early 19th century New England.

Javernick, Ellen. *What If Everybody Did That?* Children's Press. Chicago. 1990.
Summary: A child who drops a can out the car window, talks during story time, splashes at the pool, and commits other transgressions is constantly asked: "What if everybody did that?"

Keats, Exra Jack. *John Henry: An American legend.*
Summary: This is the old story of the steel-driving man, who while building the railroad, died with his hammer in his hand.

Oakley, Graham. *The Foxbury Force.* Antheneum. New York. 1994.
Summary: The Foxbury Constabulary practiced catching the Town Burglars each week to show the townspeople how good they were. All went well until the Burglars decided to keep the treasure.

Parish, Peggy, illustrated by Steven Kellog. *Granny and the Desperadoes.* Mcmillan Company. London. 1970.
Summary: Feisty Granny makes the desperadoes sorry they ever met her.

Scarry, Richard. *Pleasant Pig and the Terrible Dragon.* Random House. New York. 1980.
Summary: When Princess Lily is captured, Pleasant Pig and Lowly Worm rescue her and return law and order.

Scarry, Richard. *The Great Mystery Book.* Random House. New York. 1969.
Summary: Two stories tell how Dudley and Sam help enforce the law.

BRAVERY/COURAGE

Balder, Gaby, illustrated by Ferhard Oberlander, *Joba and the Wild Boar.* Hastings House Publishers. New York. 1961.
Summary: English and German text are side by side. Joba finds a baby boar on her doorstep. She raises it as a pet. One day she rides into the forest on the back of her boar and is lost. Her brother, Chris, shows bravery when he finds her.

Benchley, Nathaniel, illustrated by Mischa Ricter. *The Deep Dives of Stanley Whale*. Harper & Row. New York. 1973.
Summary: Stanley the young whale was small, but when he was needed to save his Uncle Moby, he found the courage to do it.

Blegvad, Lenore, illustrated by Erik Bledfvad. *Anna Banana and Me*. A Margaret K. Book. Atheneum. New York. 1985
Summary: Anna Banana's fearlessness inspires a playmate to face his own fears.

Bornstein, Ruth. *Jim*. A Clarion Book, the Seabury Press. New York. 1978.
Summary: When Jim, the dog, searches for his father who has not returned from a day of exploring, he discovers more than he expects.

Bunting, Eve, illustrated by Donald Carrick. *Ghost's Hour, Spook's Hour*. Clarion Books. New York. 1987.
Summary: Scary incidents at midnight give Biff, the dog, and his master a frightening time but all turn out to have explanations.

Carlson, Nancy. *Harriet and the Roller Coaster*. Carolrhoda Books, Inc. Minneapolis. 1982.
Summary: Harriet accepts her friend George's challenge to ride the roller coaster and finds out that she is the brave one.

Church, Kristine, illustrated by Kilmeny Niland. *My Brother John*. Tambourine Books. New York. 1990.
Summary: A younger sister describes her almost fearless older brother.

Conford, Ellen, illustrated by John Larrecq. *Eugene the Brave*. Little, Brown and Company. Bost. Toronto. London. 1978.
Summary: Eugene, the possum, hopes to escape his fear of the dark by sleeping all night. His sister, Geraldine, tries to help.

De Beers, Hans. *The Polar Bear and the Brave Little Hare*. North-South Books. New York. 1992.
Summary: Lars, the polar bear, teases his friend, Hugo, the hare, for being afraid of everything until the day they get lost in the snow.

Fuchshuber, Annegert. *Giant Story of Half Picture Book*. Carolrhoda Books, Inc. Minneapolis. 1988
Summary: A lonely dormouse who cannot find a friend and a giant who is an outcast from a forest society find solace in each other's company. Each character begins his story from his own half of the book and they meet in the middle.

Grifalconi, Ann. *Darkness and the Butterfly*. Little, Brown, and Company. Boston. Toronto. London. 1987.
Summary: Small Osa is fearless during the day, climbing trees and exploring the African valley where she lives, but at night she becomes afraid of the strange and terrifying things that might be in the dark.

Harris, Leon, illustrated by Joseph Schindelman. *The Great Diamond Robbery*. Antheneum. New York. 1985.
Summary: Maurice the French Mouse takes up residence in an American department store and repays their hospitality by foiling a diamond robbery.

Hayes, Sarah and Helen Craig. *This is the Bear and the Scary Night*. Little, Brown, and Company. Boston. Toronto. London. 1992.
Summary: The boy forgets his bear on a park bench. The bear has many adventures before the boy finds him the next day.

Heide, Florence Parry and Roxanne Heide Pierce, illustrated by Barbara Lehman. *Timothy Twinge*. Lothrop, Lee & Shephard Books. New York. 1993.
Summary: Timothy Twinge, a fearful worrier, discovers his own bravery after meeting an unusual visitor.

Hoban, Illian, *Arthur's Loose Tooth*. Harper & Row, Publishers, Inc. New York. 1985
Summary: Arthur, the chimp, is a little worried about losing his loose tooth, until his sister and their baby-sitter show him the real meaning of courage.

Lagercrantz, Rose and Samuel, pictures by Eva Erikson (adapted from the Swedish by Jack Perlutsky). *Brave Little Pete of Geranium Street*. Greenwillow Books. New York. 1984. 1986.
Summary: When he finally gets the cake he believes will make him strong, Pete becomes brave enough to face two bullies.

Lewis, Rob. *Friska the Sheep That Was Too Small*. Farrar Straus Girous. New York. 1987.
Summary: Friska did not grow as the other sheep. She tried to disguise her smallness, until one day she was able to save the whole flock.

Little, Jean, illustrated by Janet Wilson. *Jess Was the Brave One*. Viking. New York. 1991.
Summary: Jess was younger, but she was braver than her sister Claire, until one day Claire proved how brave she really was.

Locker, Thomas, retold by Lenny Hort. *The Boy Who Held Back the Sea*. Dial books. New York. 1987.
Summary: By blocking the leaking hole in the dike, a young boy saves his town from destruction.

Nash, Ogden, illustrated by James Marshall. *The Adventures of Isabel*. Little, Brown, and Company. Boston. Toronto. London. 1963.
Summary: The feisty Isabel defeats giants, witches, and other threatening creatures with ease.

Nash, Ogden, illustrated by Linell. *Custard the Dragon*. Little, Brown, and Company. Boston. Toronto. London. 1959.
Summary: Belinda and her pets think they are the bravest, and Custard the Dragon is a coward, until a pirate threatens them. This classic is told in verse.

Riley, Susan. *What Does It Mean, AFRAID?* The Child's World, Inc. Elgin, Illinois. 1978
Summary: This book discusses fears that are common to children; such as the fear of the dark, heights, doctors, storms, and doing things for the first time, such as going to school.

Wells, Rosemary. *Shy Charles*. Dial Books for Young Readers. New York. 1988.
Summary: Being painfully timid and shy does not keep a young mouse from rescuing his baby-sitter in an emergency situation.

THANKFULNESS/GENEROSITY

Aliki. *Hush Little Baby:* A Folk Lullaby. Prentice-Hall, Inc. Englewood Cliffs, NH
Summary: This is the old lullaby that lists all the gifts for baby. It is beautifully illustrated.

Guzzo, Sandra E., illustrated by Kath Parkinson. *Fox and Heggis*. Albert Whitman & Company. Niles, Illinois. 1983
Summary: Fox wants to buy a special hat, but his generosity to his friends keeps him from getting it. They find the exact right way to thank him.

Hallinan, P.K. *I'm Thankful Each Day!* Children's Press. Chicago. 1988.
Summary: Beautiful illustrations and poems show a child taking time to enjoy the things he appreciates.

Lionni, Leon. *Tico and the Golden Wings*. Pantheon. New York. 1964.
Summary: A bird is born with no wings, but instead is given golden ones by the wishing bird. He loses his friends to envy until he proves himself to be generous.

McDonnell, Janet, illustrated by Linda Hohag. *Thankfulness*. Children's Press. Chicago. 1988.
Summary: Describes the feeling we call thankfulness and the things that can make us thankful.

Moncure, Janet Belk, illustrated by Frances Hook. *I Never Say I'm Thankful, But I Am*. The Child's World. Elgin, Illinois. 1979.
Summary: A child thinks aloud about all the things for which he is grateful.

Numeroff, Laura Joffe, illustrated by Felicia Bond. *If You Give A Moose a Muffin*.
Summary: Chaos can ensue if you give a moose a muffin and start him on a cycle of requests.

Paxton, Tom, illustrated by Robert Tayevsky. *Aesop's Fables*. Morrow Junior Books. New York. 1988.
Summary: This is a retelling of Aesop's fables, it is done in rhyme, with interesting pictures.

Paxton, Tom, illustrated by Robert Tayevsky. *Andocles and the Lion, and Other Aesop's Fables*. Morrow Junior Books. New York. 1991.
Summary: This is a retelling, in verse, of several of the Aesop classics.

Reece, Colleen L., illustrated by Gwen Connelly. *Saying Thank You*. The Child's World. Elgin, Illinois. 1982.
Summary: This book uses rhymes to tell of times that saying thank you makes you feel good.

Riehecky, Janet. *"Thank You"*. Children's Press. Chicago. 1989.
Summary: Describes various situations that saying "thank you" is the right thing to do.

Williams, Vera B. *A Chair for My Mother*. Greenwillow Books. New York. 1982.
Summary: A child, her waitress mother, and her grandmother save dimes to buy a comfortable armchair after all their furniture is lost in a fire.

Wolkstein, Diane, illustrated by Marc Brown. *The Banza. Dial Books* for Young Readers. New York. 1981.
Summary: This is a Haitian story of a little goat who finds that the gift of a young tiger gives her a brave heart.

TRUTHFULNESS/HONESTY

Aliki. *Diogenes*. Prentice-Hall. Englewood Cliffs, NJ
Summary: The story of the Greek philosopher, Diogenes, who spends his life looking for an honest man.

Anderson, Hans Christian, illustrated by Karl Lagerfield. *The Emperor's New Clothes*. Atlantic Monthly Press. New York, 1992.
Summary: The old story of how only a child was honest enough to tell the emperor that he was naked, after he had been bilked by dishonest tailors.

Avi, illustrated by Matthew Henry. *The Bird, the Frog, and the Light*. Orchard Books. New York. 1994.
Summary: A frog learns the truth about his self-importance when he meets a bird whose simple song brings the sun's light to the world.

Berry, Joy Wilt, illustrated by John Costanza. *Let's Talk About Cheating*. Children's Press. Chicago. 1985.
Summary: This book discusses what happens when children cheat.

Berenstain, Stan and Jan. *The Berenstain Bears and the Truth*. Random House. New York. 1983.
Summary: Brother and Sister Bear learn how important it is to tell the truth after they accidnetally break Mama Bear's favorite lamp.

Blue, Rose, illustrated by Laura Hartman. *Wishful Lying*. Human Science Press. New York. 1980.
Summary: Convinced that they don't care about him, a little boy makes up stories about all the things he and his parents do together.

Brown, Marc. *The True Francine*. Little, Brown and Company. Boston. Toronto. London. 1981.
Summary: Francine and Muffy are good friends until Muffy lets Francine take the blame for cheating on a test.

Carlson, Nancy. *Arnie and the Stolen Markers*. Viking Kestrel. New York. 1987.
Summary: After spending his allowance at Harvey's Toy Shop, Arnie steals a set of markers.

Carlson, Nancy. *Harriet and the Garden*. Carolrhoda Books, Inc. Minneapolis. 1982.
Summary: Harriet feels terrible until she confesses to trampling on a neighbor's garden and ruining a prize dahlia.

Demi. *The Empty Pot*. Henry Holt and Company. New York. 1990.
Summary: All the other children bring wonderful plants to the emperor. Only one honest child brings an empty pot.

Elliot, Dan, illustrated by Joe Mathieu. *Ernie's Little Lie*. Random House/Children's Television Workshop. New York. 1983.
Summary: Ernie enters a painting by his cousin Fred in a contest in order to win a box of paints.

Gretz, Susanna. *Rabbit Ramble On*. Four Winds Press. New York. 1992.
Summary: Duck and Frog decide to teach boastful Rabbit a lesson.

Havill, Juanita, illustrated by Anne Sibley O'Brian. *Jamaica's Find*. Houghton-Mifflin Company. 1986.
Summary: A little girl finds a stuffed dog in the park and decides to take it home.

Moncure, Janet Belk, illustrated by Paul Karch. *HONESTY: What is It?* The Child's World. Elgin, Illinois. 1980.
Summary: Examples from daily life that characterize honesty.

Moss, Marissa. *Who Was It?* Houghton-Mifflin Company. Boston, 1989.
Summary: After Isabelle breaks the cookie jar, she an her brother invent a variety of wild stories to explain the damage to their mother.

Nielsen, Shelley, illustrated by Virginia Kyberg. *Telling the Truth*. Abdo and Daughters. Edina, Minnesota. 1992.
Summary: Poems present situations why telling the truth is important.

Sharmat, Marjorie illustrated by David McPhail. *A Big Fat Enourmous Lie*. E. P. Dutton. New York. 1978.
Summary: A child's simple lie grows to enormous proportions.

FAIRNESS/SPORTSMANSHIP

Baehr, Patricia, illustrated by R.W. Alley. *School Isn't Fair*. Four Winds Press. New York. 1989
Summary: Four-year-old Edward describes all the unfair things that happen to him during a school day.

Berenstain, Stan and Jan. *The Berenstain Bears Ready, Set, Go!* Random House. New York. 1988.
Summary: The Berenstain Bears compete in sports. This is a First time Reader that teaches comparatives.

Berry, Joy Wilt, illustrated by John Costanza. *Let's Talk About Being A Bad Sport*. Children's Press. Chicago. 1986.
Summary: The first half of the book talks of behaviors of bad sports. The second half shows how good sports act.

Dale, Penny. *Bet You Can't*. J.B. Lippincott. New York. 1987.
Summary: At bedtime, sister and brother engage in a bout of challenges as they tidy their room.

Galdone, Paul. *The Monkey and the Crocodile*. Houghton-Mifflin. Clarion Books. New York. 1969.
Summary: This is a retelling of a Jatakas, an Indian fable, about how the clever monkey out-smarts the hungry crocodile.

Harper, Anita, illustrated by Susan Hellard. *It's Not Fair*. G. P. Putnam's Sons. New York. 1986.
Summary: When a new baby brother kangaroo got all the attention his sister did not think it was fair. Later she learned that he would grow up to say the same words to her.

Hautzig, Deborah, illustrated by Tom Leigh. *It's Not Fair!* Random House. Children's Television Workshop. New York. 1986.
Summary: When irresponsible Ernie seems to be taking all the credit for Bert's hard work on their lemonade stand, it provokes an angry outburst from Bert and threatens their friendship.

Hines, Anna Grossnickle. *Keep Your Old Hat*. E.P. Dutton. New York. 1987.
Summary: Young children playing, learn the necessity of compromise.

Holabird, Katharine, illustrated by Helen Craig. *Angelina and Alice*. Clarkson N. Potter, Inc. Publishers. New York. 1987.
Summary: Angelina and her best friend Alice discover the importance of teamwork when their acrobatics are the hit of the gymnastics show at the village fair.

Isenbery, Barbara and Susan Wolf, illustrated by Diane De Groat. *Albert the Running Bear Gets the Jitters*. Clarion Books. New York. 1987.
Summary: Albert has won all his races, but when he is challenged by Boris the bully he suffers stress. Good sportsmanship pays off for both of them.

Kessler, Leonard. *Old Turtle's Soccer Team*. Greenwillow Books. New York. 1988.
Summary: Under Old Turtle's guidance, the animals learn how to play soccer and the meaning of good sportsmanship.

Nielsen, Shelly, illustrated by Virginia Kylbert. *Playing Fair*. Abdo and Daughters. Minneapolis. 1992.
Summary: Brief rhymes present occasions when fairness is needed in dealing with friends, bullies, games, groups, and tests.

Palisciano, Diane. *Garden Partners*. Atheneum. New York. 1989.
Summary: A child and her grandmother plant seeds, care for their garden all summer, and share the harvest with friends and family.

Sarnoff, Jane and Reynold Ruffins. *That's Not Fair*. Charles Scribner's Sons. New York. 1980.
Summary: Becky thinks her old brother has the best of things in their family and "that's not fair".

Schultz, Charles M. *You're Good Sport, Charlie Brown*. Random House. New York. 1976.
Summary: Charlie and hsi friends take part in a motor cross.

Steptoe, John. *Mufaro's Beautiful Daughters, An African Tale*. Lothrop, Lee & Shepard Books. New York. 1987.
Summary: Mufaro's two beautiful daughters, one bad-tempered, and one kind and sweet, go before the king who is choosing a wife.

Young, Karen Roman, illustrated by Doug Cushman. *Excuse Me, But It's My Turn*. Children's Press. Chicago. 1963.
Summary: A Best Behavior Series book. A child's guide to good sport's manners.

Zolotow, Charlotte, illustrated by Arnold Lobel. *The Quarreling Book*. Harper & Row, Publishers. New York. 1963.
Summary: Everyone is having a bad, rainy day, accusing each other unfairly, until the sun comes out again.

POLITENESS/COURTESY

Alden, Laura, illustrated by Dan Siculan. *Saying I'm Sorry*. The Child's World. Elgin, Illinois. 1982
Summary: Rhyming text and illustrations present a variety of situations where an apology is required.

Barnett, Ada, Pam Manquen and Linda Rapaport, illustrations by Mark Hoffman. *Eddycat Introduces Mannersville*. Gareth Stevens Publishin. Milwaukee. 1993.
Summary: When Buddy Brownbear moves to Mannersville, he finds the entire town full of friendly, polite animals who know how to behave properly. At various intervals in the text, Eddycat makes additional comments about etiquette.

Barnett, Ada, Pam Manquen and Linda Rapaport, illustrations by Mark Hoffman, *Eddycat Teaches Telephone Skills*. Gareth Stevens Publishing. Milwaukee. 1993
Summary: Father Brownbear helps Buddy learn how to use the telephone correctly and politely. At intervals in the story, Eddycat gives additional advice on practicing telephone etiquette.

Behrens, June, photographs by Michele and Tomm Grimm. *The Manners Book*. Children's Press. Chicago. 1980.
Summary: Chris' stuffed bear Ned answers questions about the proper thing to do in a number of social situations.

Berenstain, Stan and Jan. *The Berenstain Bears Forget Their Manners*. Random House. New York. 1985.
Summary: Mama Bear comes up with a plan to correct the Bear family's rude behavior.

Berry, Joy Wilt, illustrated by John Costanza. *Let's Talk About Being Rude*. Children's Press. Chicago. 1985.
Summary: The book discusses rude and polite behavior.

Brown, Marc and Stephen Krensky. *Perfect Pigs, An Introduction to Manners*. Little, Brown and Company. Boston. Toronto. 1983.
Summary: A simple introduction to good manners to use with family, friends, at school, during meals, with pets, on the phone, during games, at parties, and in public places.

Chapman, Cheryl, illustrated by Susan L.Roth. *Pass the Fritters Critters*. Four Winds Press. New York. 1993.
Summary: Hungry animals passing food during a meal learn that "please" is a magic word.

Hoban, Russell, illustrated by James Marshall, *Dinner at Alberta's*. Thomas Y. Crowell Company. New York. 1975.
Summary: Arthur Crocodile cannot seem to learn table manners until his sister brings her new girlfriend to visit.

Howe, James, illustrated by Peter Elwell. *The Muppet Guide to Magnificent Manners*. Muppet Press/Random House. 1984.
Summary: An amusing, advanced book of manners and the reasons for them in many different situations.

Joslin, Sesyle, illustrated by Maurice Sendak. *What Do You Say, Dear?* Addison-Weley. Reading, MA 1958.
Summary: A guide for good manners in many silly and wonderful situations.

Moncure, Jane Belk, illustrated by Nancy Inderieden. *Saying Please.* The Child's World. Elgin, Illinois. 1982.
Summary: Presents situations in which using the word "please" is effective.

Moncure, Jane Belk, illustrated by Lois Axeman. *Please...Thanks...I'm Sorry!* The Child's World. Elgin, Illinois. 1985.
Summary: An introduction to basic etiquette in rhymed text with illustrations.

Nielsen, Shelly, illustrated by Marie-Claude Monchaux. *Manners*. Abdo & Daughters. Minneapolis. 1992.
Summary: Poems feature good etiquette being practiced.

Parrish, Peggy, illustrated by Marylin Hafner. *Mind Your Manners*. Greenwillow Books. New york. 1978
Summary: An introduction to proper manners for meeting new people, receiving gifts, using the telephone, dining out, and other common social situations.

Riehecky, Janet, illustrated by Gwen Connelly. *"EXCUSE ME"*. Children's Press. Chicago. 1989.
Summary: Describes various situations in which it is appropriate to say, "Excuse me."

Riehecky, Janet, illustrated by Gwen Connelly. *"I'M SORRY"*. The Child's World, Inc. USA. 1989.
Summary: Describes various situations in which it is appropriate to say, "I'm sorry".

Riehecky, Janet, illustrated by Gwen Connelly. *"After You"*. The Child's World, Inc. USA. 1989.
Summary: Describes various situations in which it is appropriate to say, "After you".

Riehecky, Janet, illustrated by Gwen Connelly. *"Thank You"*. The Child's World, Inc. USA. 1989.
Summary: Describes various situations in which it is appropriate to say, "Thank You".

Scarry, Richard. *Please and Thank You Book*. Random House. New York. 1973
Summary: A charming collection of stories that teach good manners.

Slobodkin, Louis, *Excuse Me! Certainly*. Vanguard Press, Inc. New York. 1959.
Summary: Willie White learns to be polite. Story told in rhyme.

Young, Karen Roman, illustrated by Doug Cushman. *Excuse Me, You're Standing in Front of the TV*. Childrens Press. Chicago. 1986.
Summary: Tells of good manners needed at home. A Best Behavior Series Book.

Young, Karen Roman, illustrated by Doug Cushman. *Excuse Me, May I Have an Extra Napkin?*. Childrens Press. Chicago. 1986.
Summary: A charming bunny explains good manners while eating in different situations.. A Best Behavior Series Book.

Young, Karen Roman, illustrated by Doug Cushman. *Please, May I Have a Pencil?* Children's Press. Chicago. 1986.
Summary: A Best Behavior Series book. A child's guide to party manners.

Young, Karen Roman, illustrated by Doug Cushman. *Excuse Me, But It's My Turn...*Children's Press. Chicago. 1986.
Summary: A Best Behavior book. A child's guide to sports manners.

COOPERATION/HELPFULNESS

Acona, George, *Helping Out*. Clarion Books. Ticknor & Fields. A Houghton-Mifflin Company. New York. 1985.
Summary: Explores in black and white photographs the special relationship between adults and children working together in many different settings.

Bos, Joan W., illustrated by Emily Arnold McCully. *The Grandpa Days*. Simon and Schuster Books for Young Readers. New york. 1989
Summary: Philip comes up with just the right project to build with Grandpa during their week together, but first he has to learn the differnce between wishes and good planning.

Bradman, Tony and Joanna Burroughes. *Not Like That, Like This!* Oxford University Press. New York. 1988.
Summary: Dad and Thomas go for a walk. They start to tease about how to stick their heads through the iron railings of a fence. Everyone has to cooperate to get Dad unstuck.

Buerger, Jane, illustrated by Jennie Davis. *HELPING, What Is It?* The Child's World. Elgin, Illinois. 1984.
Summary: Shows ways a child can be helpful to family and friends.

Cowen-Fletcher, Jane. *It Takes a Village*. Scholastic, Inc. New York. 1994.
Summary: On market day in a small village in Benen, Yemi tries to watch her little brother Kokou and finds that the entire village is watching out for him too.

Denslow, Sharon Phillips, illustrated by Nancy Carpenter. *At Taylor's Place*. 1990.
Summary: Tory helps her friend Taylor with projets including a weathervane for Miss Perry, topped with a carved figure of her dog, Marvin.

Hautzig, Deborah, illustrated by Joe Mathieu. *It's Easy*. Random House/Children's Television Workshop. New York. 1988
Summary: Big Bird regrets his decision not to let any of his friends help him plant his sunflower seeds when a flock of birds try to eat his flowers.

Hughes, Shirley. *Alfie Gives a Hand*. Lothrop, Lee & Shepard Books. New York. 1983
Summary: When Alfie is invited to a birthday party without his mother or sister, he finds that he must put down his security blanket to be able to be helpful.

Lobel, Arnold. *Frog and Toad Together*. Harper & Row. New York. 1971, 1972.
Summary: These five stories tell of the friends adventures.

Martin, Jacqueline Briggs, illustrated by Stella Ormai. *Bizzy Bones and the Lost Quilt*. Lothrop, Lee & Shepard Books. New York. 1988.
Summary: When Bizzy loses the quilt he needs to go to sleep, Uncle Ezra and the orchard mice try to make him a new one.

Morgan, Michaela, illustrated by Moira Kemp. *Helpful Betty to the Rescue*. Carolrhoda Books, Inc. Minneapolis, 1993.
Summary: Betty the hippo rushes to rescue a monkey she thinks is stuck up a tree.

Morgan Michaela, illustrated by Moira Kemp. *Helpful Betty Solves a Mystery*. Carolrhoda Books, Inc. Minneapolis. 1993.
Summary: Betty the hippo finds a magnifying glass and goes off to find a mystery to go with it.

Riehecky, Janet, illustrated by Kathryn Hutton. *Cooperation, Values to Live By*. The Child's World. Chicago, Illinois. 1990.
Summary: Shows why cooperation is so important.

Ross, Tony. *Stone Soup*. A Puffin Pied Piper. New York. 1987.
Summary: A new version of the old classic. Mother Hen is going to be in the soup herself, unless she can trick the Big Bad Wolf.

Walter, Mildred Pitts, illustred by Pat Cummings. *Two and Too Much*. Bradbury Press. New York. 1990
Summary: Brandon is seven and he offers to watch his two-year-old sister, Gina, while his mother gets ready for a party. He soon finds he has his hands full.

Valthuijs, Max. *Elephant and Crocodile*. Farrar, Straus and Girroux. New York. 1990.
Summary: Elephant must listen to his neighbor, Crocodile, practice his violin day after day, and far into the night. Elephant decides to learn to play the trumpet. The noise is awful. Finally they learn to cooperate and make music together.

CHEERFULNESS/JOY

Butcher, Julia. *The Sheep and the Rowan Tree*. Hold, Rinhard and Winston. New York. 1984.
Summary: The rowan tree is discontented until a bird who has been around the world convinces it that it is best where it is.

Carlson, Nancy. *Life is Fun!* Viking Kestrel. New York. 1993.
Summary: Wonderful pictures and text accent all the good things that make life fun.

Carolson, Nancy. **I Like Me!** Viking Kestrel. New York. 1988.
Summary: By admiring her finer points and showing that she can take care of herself and have fun even when there's no one else around, a charming pig proves the best friend you can have is yourself.

Clark, Emma Chichester. *Across the Blue Mountains*. Gulliver Books. Harcourt Brace & Company. San Diego. 1993.
Summary: Miss Bilberry is happy in her little yellow house, but she wonders what is on the other side of the mountain. She travels to discover that home is where her heart is.

Greene, Carol, illustrated by Gene Sharp. *Shine, Sun!* Children's Press. Chicago. 1983.
Summary: This is a Rookie Reader that shows a child's happy reaction to the sun.

Hillerty, Margaret, illustrated by Robert Masheris. *Away Go the Boats.* Follett Publishing Company. Chicago. 1981.
Summary: This is an easy to read book that shows how a littel girl's imagination allows her to travel to wonderful places.

Hirshi, Ron, photographs by Thomas D. Mangelsen. *A Time for Singing.* Cobblehill Books. Dutton. 1994.
Summary: Beautiful color photographs of birds and animals and their various reasons for using their voices.

Locker, Thomas. *Miranda's Smile.* Dial Books. New York. 1994.
Summary: Miranda's artist father wants to paint her smile just so, finally he finds a way, even though she has just lost her front tooth.

McCarthy, Bobette. *Happy Hiding Hippos.* Bradbury Press. New York. 1994.
Summary: An easy to read, beautifully illustrated, book of a happy hippo family playing hide and seek.

Moncure, Jane Belk, illustrated by Pat Karch. *JOY What is It?* Children's Press. Chicago. 1982.
Summary: This book tells of all the times that a child can have happy feelings.

Moncure, Jane Belk, illustrated by Linda Hohag. *"Smile," Says Little Crocodile.* Children's Press. Chicago. 1988.
Summary: Little Crocodile likes to smile, and shows all the good things a child can do to stay healthy and happy.

Piatti, Celestina. *The Happy Owls.* Atheneum. New York. 1963.
Summary: This is a beautiful classic, a retold legend of a pair of owls that remain happy while all around them others are fighting.

Scheffler, Ursel, illustrated by Jutta Timm. *Sun Jack and Rain Jack.* Gareth Stevens Publishing, Milwaukee. 1994.
Summary: Half of the book shows ways Jack can be happy in the rain, turn the book over and it shows how he is happy in the sun.

Simon, Norma, illustrated by Helen Congancherry. *I Am Not A Crybaby.* Albert Whitman & Company. Niles, Illinois. 1989.
Summary: Children in different situations talk about when they cry, or feel like crying. It is explained to be a normal reaction.

Steig, William. *Spinky Sulks.* Michael di Capua Books; Farrar, Straus, and Giroux. New York. 1988.
Summary: Spinky is angry with his entire family. Nothing they can do cheers him, until he decides to give them a surprise.

Tapio, Pat Decker, illustrated by Paul Galdone. *The Lady Who Saw the Good in Everything.* A Clarion Book. The Seabury Press. New York. 1975.
Summary: A woman's blithe spirit never wavers, despite the growing disasters that sweep her and her cat from their comfortable home and carry them half-way around the world.

Thaler, Mike, illustrated by Tracey Cameron. *The Clown's Smile.* Harper and Row. New York, 1962, 1986.
Summary: An elusive smile flies from clown to acrobat to lion tamer to other people at the circus, until the clown's crying prompts it to return.

Vincent, Gabrielle. *Smile, Ernest and Celestine.* Greenwillow Books. New York. 1982.
Summary: After he explains to Celestine why his collection of photographs does not include her, Ernest remedies the omission.

Waddell, Martin, illustrated by Jill Barton. *The Happy Hedgehog Band.* Candlewick Press. Cambridge. MA. 1991.
Summary: The hedgehogs have so much fun with their band that all the animals of the forest join them.

Wiethorn, Randall J. *Rock Finds a Friend.* The Green Tiger Press, Inc. San Diego. 1988.
Summary: A small rock is lonely until he stops a young boy from using him to hurt others. They become friends and are happy together.

INITIATIVE/READINESS

Aliki. *A Weed is a Flower: The Life of George Washington Carver.* Prentice-Hall, Inc. Englewood Clifs, NJ 1965.
Summary: The hard times and great success of George Washington Carver.

Aseltine, Lorraine, illustrated by Virginia Wright-Frierson. *First Grade Can Wait.* Albert Whitman & Company. Niles, Illinois. 1988.
Summary: Luke is fearful of first grade. His teacher and parents decide it is better to wait one more year.

Barton, Byron. *I Want To Be An Astronaut.* Thoms Y. Crowell. New York. 1988.
Summary: A young child wants to be an astronaut and goes on a mission into space.

Brandenber, Franz, illustrated by ALIKI. *Everyone Ready!* Greenwillow Books. New York, 1979.
Summary: The Field Mouse family is trying to take a trip together, but they have trouble all being ready at the same time.

Graham, Al, illustrated by Tony Palazzo. *Timothy Turtle.* The Viking Press. New York. 1946.
Summary: Timothy Turtle was living a good life, but he wanted to be famous. He proved himself by climbing to Took-a-Look Hill.

Gramatky, Hardi. *Little Toot.* G.P. Putnam's Sons. New York, 1939. 1967.
Summary: Little Toot, the tugboat, liked to play, until he had to use his initiative to save the big boats.

Greaves, Margaret, illustrated by Teresa O'Brien. *Henry's Wild Morning.* Dial Books for Young Readers. New York. 1991.
Summary: Henry, the kitten, the smallest in the litter, pretends he is as big and brave as a tiger. This book is enriched with beautiful illustrations.

Isadora, Rachel. *Ben's Trumpet.* Greenwillow Books. New York. 1979.
Summary: Ben wants to be a trumpeter, but plays only an imaginary instrument until one of the musicians in a neighborhood night club discovers his ambition. (Caldecott Honor Book, Reading Rainbow selection).

Kuklin, Susan. *When I See My Dentist...* Bradbury Press. New York. 1988.
Summary: Alicia goes to the dentist. This story is told with photographs and gives much important information.

Kuklin, Susan. *When I See My Doctor...*Bradbury Press. New York. 1988
Summary: Thomas goes to the doctor for a check up. This story is told with wonderful photographs and easy to understand explanations of the parts of a physical exam.

Lasky, Kathryn, illustrated by Bobette McCarthy. *The Solo*. Mcacmillan Publishing Company. New York. 1994.
Summary: When she is excluded from the group dance, a little girl insists to her family that she is going to dance a solo at her school's spring concert-with the entire air force in the audience.

Long, Earlene, pictures by Neal Slavin and Charles Mikolaycak. *Johnny's Eggs*. Addison-Wesley, Reading, Mass. 1980.
Summary: Relates how a little boy successfully breaks his own egg for breakfast.

McPhail, David. *Andrew's Bath*. Little, Brown and Company. Boston. 1984.
Summary: Andrew makes giving himself a bath for the first time an adventure.

Miller, Margaret. *Where's Jenna?* Simon and Schuster Books for Young Readers. New York. 1994.
Summary: Jenna uses her initiative to stay one step ahead of her mother at bath time. The story is told with wonderful photographs. Prepositions are highlighted.

Ichikawa, Satomi, story by Patricia Lee Gauch. *Dance, Tanya*. Philomel Books. New York. 1989.
Summary: Tanya loves ballet bancing, repeating the moves she sees her older sister doing when practicing for class or a recital, and soon Tanya is big enough to go to ballet class herself.

Lester, Helen, illustrated by Lynn Munsinger. *Tacky the Penguin*. Houghton mifflin Company. Boston. 1988.
Summary: Tacky the penguin does not fit in with his sleek and graceful companions, but his odd behavior comes in handy when hunters come with maps and ropes.

McPhail, David. *Pig Pig Gets a Job*. Dutton Children's Books. New York. 1990
Summary: Pig Pig thinks of all the jobs he could get, from cook to auto mechanic. He is enthusiastic about performing similar tasks for his family at home.

Mason, Margo, illustrated by Caterhine Siracusa. *Ready, Alice?* A Bantam Little Rooster Book. New York. 1990.
Summary: Alice takes her time getting up , getting dressed, eating breakdfast, and getting ready for the beach.

Parish, Peggy, illustrated by Leonar Kessler. *Be Ready at Eight*. Macmillan Publishing Co., Inc. New York. 1979.
Summary: Mis Molly has a string tied around her finger to remind her to be ready at eight, she just can't remember what she is to be ready for.

Sadler, Marilyn, illustrated by Roger Bollen. *Alistair's Time Machine*. Simon and Schuster Books for Young Readers. New Yrok. 1986.
Summary: Alistair is a boy of science. He is surprised when his unreliable time machine doesn't win first prize in the Science Fair.

Skutina, Bladimir and Marie-Jose Sacre. *Nobody Has Time for Me*. Wellington Publishing. Chicago. 1988.
Summary: Karin meets a person she thinks is Father Time and learns how people use their time in many different ways.

Urdry, Janice May, illustrated by Karen Gundersheimer. *Is Susan Here?* Harper Collins, Publishers. New York. 1962, 1993.
Summary: Susan uses her initiative to be different animals all day. Finally she and her parents decide they miss Susan.

Ziefert, Harriet, illustrated by Mavis Smith. *Harry Gets Ready for School.* Viking New York. 1991
Summary: Harry the hippo gets ready to start school.

NEATNESS/CLEANLINESS

Berestain, Stan and Jan. *The Berestain Bears and the Messy Room.* Random House. New York. 1983
Summary: The entire Bear family becomes involved in an attempt to clean and organize the cub's messy room.

Berry, Joy, illustrated by John Costanza. *Let's Talk About Being Messy.* Children's Press. Chicago. 1986.
Summary: Discusses messy habits and neat ones.

Berry, Joy, illustrated by Bartholomew. *Teach Me About Bathtime.* Children's Press. Chicago. 1985.
Summary: Describes the steps in taking a bath.

Berry, Joy, illustrated by John Costanza. *Let's Talk About Being Messy*. Children's Press. Chicago. 1986
Summary: Discusses the do's and don'ts of being messy or neat.

Bottner, Barbara. *Messy.* Delacorte Press. New York. 1979.
Summary: A six-year-old girl has a difficult time being neat.

Cummings, Pat. *Clean Your Room, Harvey Moon!* Bradbury Press. New York. 1991.
Summary: Harvey tackles a big job: cleaning his room

DePaola, Tomie. *Marianna May and Nursey.* Holiday House. New York. 1983.
Summary: Marianna May was not having a good time wearing white dresses and staying clean all the time, until the servants solved the problem.

Dowling, Paul. *You Need a Bath, Mustard.* Hyperion Books for Children. New York. 1993.
Summary: A book for 1-5 year-olds. Teddy bear gets a bubble bath from his friends.

Erskine, Jim. *Bert and Susie's Messy Tale.* Crown Publishers, Inc. New York. 1979.
Summary: Bert has problems getting his mother's chrysanthemum to the flower show.

Gantos, Jack, illustrated by Nicole Rubel. *Swampy Alligator.* Windmill/Wanderer Books. New York. 1980.
Summary: Swampy likes to be smelly and dirty until his friends give him a birthday surprise: a bubble bath.

Gretz, Susanna. *It's Your Turn, Roger!* Dial Books for Young Readers. New York. 1986
Summary: Roger thinks his family is too fussy, until he has a chance to see how some others live.

Gretz, Susanna. *Roger Loses His Marbles!* Dial Books for Young Readers. New York. 1988.
Summary: When Aunt Lulu pays a visit, she stays in Roger's room and tidies it up, which makes him mad until she finds something Roger had lost.

Hamso, Bobbie, illustrations by Paul Sharp. *Dirty Larry.* Children's Press. Chicago. 1983.
Summary: Larry gets dirty, but he also enjoys taking a shower at the end of the day (This is a Rookie Reader book.)

Hickman, Martha Whitmare, illustrated by Mary Alice Baer. *Eeps Creeps, It's My Room!* Abingdon Press. Nashville. 1984.
Summary: Jefferey hates to clean his room, but once he begins he finds many lost toys, and finds it is nice to have things in order.

Howells, Mildred, illustrated by William Curtis Holdsworth. *The Woman Who Lived in Holland.* Farrar, Straus and Giroux. New York. 1973.
Summary: A favorite old story (first published in 1898) tells of a woman who went too far with her cleaning!

Hurd, Eddith Thacher, illustrated by Clement Hurd. *Stop Stop.* Harper & Row. New York. 1961.
Summary: Miss Muggs almost ruins Suzie's day when she chose to scrub and clean everyone and everything in sight, until she goet drenched herself!

Hutchins, Pat. *Tidy Titch.* Greenwillow Books. New York. 1991
Summary: Titch helps his older brother and sister clean their rooms.

Kroll, Steven, illustrated by Jeni Bassett. *The Pigrates Clean Up.* Henry Hold and Company. New York. 1993.
Summary: When the pigrates hear that the captain is to be married they must all work hard to clean themselves and their ship.

Kudrna, C. Imbior. *To Bathe A Boa.* Carolrhoda Books, Inc. Minneapolis. 1986.
Summary: The boa doesn't want a bath. The child has to use all his wits to get it into the tub.

Lindblom, Steven, illustrated by True Kelley. *Let's Give Kitty a Bath!* Addison-Wesley. Reading. MA. 1982.
Summary: Two children try to give a tricky cat a bath. They all got a surprise.

Lewis, Rob. *Tidy Up, Trevor.* Gulliver Books. Harcourt Brace Jovanovich, Publishers. San Diego. New York. London. 1993.
Summary: Although he is bored, Trevor the turtle doesn't want to join his family on a trip down the river, so he amuses himself while cleaning out his closet.

McKissick, Patricia and Frederick. *Messy Bessey.* Illustrations by Richard Hackney. Children's Press. Chicago. 1987.
Summary: Bessey finally cleans up her messy room.

McKissick, Patricia and Frederick. *Messy Bessey's Closet.* Children's Press. Chicago. 1989.
Summary: Messy Bessey learns a lesson about sharing when she cleans out her closet.

McQueen, Lucinda and Jeremy Guitar. *Tidy Pig.* Random House. New York. 1989.
Summary: Florinda Pig is upset when her family moves in and messes her house, until they see they have made her ill.

Morris, Ann, illustrated by Ruth Young. *Eleanora Mousie Makes a Mess.* Macmillan Publishing Company. New York. 1987.
Summary: Everything Eleanora Mousie does creates a mess, but she enjoys herself and makes others happy.

Peters, Lisa Westberg, pictures by Brad Sneed. *When the Fly Flew In...* Dial Books for Young Readers. New York. 1994.
Summary: The child and the animals are not interested in cleaning their room, until strange things happen when a fly flies in.

Mess. Macmillan Publishing Company. New York. 1987.
Summary: Everything Eleanor Mousie does creates a mess, but she enjoys herself and makes others happy.

Phillips, Tamara, illustrated by Dora Leder. *Day Care ABC*. Albert Whitman & Company. Niles, Illinois. 1989.
Summary: Children's names and activities are used to show the order of the alphabet.

Potter, Beatrix. *The Tale of Mrs. Tittlemouse*. Frederick Warner & Co. Inc. New York. 1910.
Summary: This classic still delights us with her desire for tidiness.

Rockwell, Anne and Harlow. *Nice and Clean*. Macmillan Publishing Company. New York. 1984.
Summary: Presents the many devices and implements from mop and broom to scouring pad and silver polish that are used in cleaning the house.

Sardegna, Jill, illustrated by Michael Hays. *K is for Kiss Good Night: A bedtime Alphabet*. A Doubleday Book for Young Readers. New York. 1994.
Summary: As the children follow the order of the alphabet, a step in getting ready for bed is given. This is a beautiful book that shows children of many cultures.

Sharmat, Mitchell, illustrated by Sue Truesdaell. *The Seven Sloppy Days of Phineas Pig*. Harcourt Brace Jovanovich, Publishers. San Diego. 1983.
Summary: Phineas Pig liked things neat. Hsi family was so digusted with his tidiness they sent him away to his uncle for sloppy lessons. It did not take him long when her returned home to find he really did like to be neat and clean.

Swartz, Mary Ada, pictures by Lynn Munsinger. Spiffen, *A Tale of a Tidy Pig*. Albert Whitman & Company. Niles, Illinois. 1988.
Summary: Spiffin, the pig spurned by the sloppy other pigs of Sloppyville, becomes a hero through a daring deed only a tidy pig could have performed.

Teague, Mark. *Pigsty*. Scholastic, Inc. New York. 1994.
Summary: When Wendell doesn't clean up his room, a whole herd of pigs come to live with him.

Wilhelm, Hans. *Oh, What A Mess*. Crown Publishers, Inc. New York. 1988.
Summary: After Franklin Pig wins first prize in an art contest, his very messy family finally begins to put their home in order.

UNIQUENESS

Aliki. *The Story of Johnny Appleseed*. Prentice-Hall Books for Young Readers. New York. 1963.
Summary: The story of how Johnny Chapman became known as Johnny Appleseed by planting apple trees and sharing seeds settlers he met.

Carey, Mary. *Owl Who Loved Sunshine*. Golden Press. New York. 1977.
Summary: Leander, the owl, loves the sunshine in the meadow and enjoys watching the animals play all day. He is then shunned as an "improper" owl. Later, he is able to prove himself as a kind friend when he fights with a weasel.

Johnson, Spencer. *Value Of Believing In Yourself: The Story of Louis Pastuer.*
Summary: An invaluable lesson is taught in this insightful story of the life of Louis Pasteur.

Williams, Barbara, illustrated by Kay Chorao. *Someday, Said Mitchell*. E.P. Dutton & Co, Inc. New York. 1976.
Summary: As Mitchell plans how he will help his mother when he grows up, she tell how he can help now while he is still little.

INDEPENDENCE

Hodgson, Harriet, *My First Fourth of July Book*. Children's Press. Chicago. 1987
Summary: Traditional celebrations of our nation's birthday are told in rhymes.

Keller, Beverly. *Pimm's Place*. Cowar, McCann & Geoghegan. New York. 1978
Summary: A timorous young boy teaches his rowdy cousins the value of being quiet and using one's imagination.

Munro, Roxie. *The Inside-Outside Book of Washington, D.C.* E.P. Dutton. New York. 1987.
Summary: Beautiful views of the inside and outside of many of the historic buildings in our nation's capital.

Pfister, Marcus. *The Rainbow Fish*. North South Books. New York. 1992.
Summary: The most beautiful fish in the entire ocean discovers the real value of personal beauty and friendship.

Rathmann, Peggy. *Ruby the Copycat*. Scholastic. New York. 1991.
Summary: Ruby insists on copying Angela, until her teacher helps her discover her own creative resources.

Ross, Tony. *Eggbert*. Putnam. New York. 1994.
Summary: A cracked egg with a talent for painting goes through some painful experiences before realizing being cracked is something to be proud of.

Smith, Dennis. *The Little Engine That Saved The City*. Doubleday. New York. 1990.
Summary: A reliable fire engine that was retired in favor of newer equipment, saves the day when the biggest fire the city has ever seen gets out of control.

RESOURCEFULNESS

Avi, Illustrated by Matthew Henry. *The Bird, the Frog, and the Light*. Orchard Books. New York. 1994
Summary: A frog learn the truth about his self-importance and he meets a bird whose simple song brings the sun's light to the world.

Brandenberg, Franz, illustrated by Aliki. *Everyone Ready?* Greenwillow Books. New York. 1979
Summary: The field mouse family is trying to take a trip together, but they have trouble all being ready at the same time.

Lester, Julius. *Sam And The Tigers*. Dial Books. New York. 1996
Summary: A little boy named Sam matches wits with several tigers who want to eat him.

Locker, Thomas, retold by Lenny Hart. *The Boy Who Held Back the Sea*. Dial Books. New York. 1987
Summary: By blocking the leaking hole in the dike, a young boy saves his town from destruction.

Silverstein, Shel. *The Giving Tree*. Harper Collins. New York. 1964.
Summary: A young boy grows to manhood experiencing the love and generosity of a tree which gives to him without thought of return.

Woerkam, Dorothy Van. *Becky and The Bear*. Putnam. New York. 1975
Summary: A young girl in colonial Maine manages to catch a bear in an unusual way.

PEACEFULNESS

Burns-Knight, Margy. *Who Belongs Here? An American Story*. Tilbury House. 1993.
Summary: After escaping from the killing fields of Cambodia and living in a refugee camp in Thailand, a ten-year-old boy must adjust to his new life in the United States.

DePaola, Tomie. *Watch Out for Chicken Feet in Your Soup*. Prentice Hall, Englewood Cliffs. NJ. 1974
Summary: A young boy gain a new appreciation for his Italian grandmother when he sees her through the eyes of his friends.

Derby, Janice, illustrated by Joy Dunn Keenan. *Are You My Friend?* Herald Press. Scottdale, PA. 1993
Summary: A child meets many people who are different, but who can still be friends.

Gantschev, Ivan. *Good Morning, Good Night*. Picture Book Studio. Saxonville, MA. 1991.
Summary: Tells how the bragging sun and the quiet moon come to be friends and to respect and value their differences.

Green, Kate, illustrated by Steve Mark. *Just About Perfect*. The Child's Word. Makato, MN. 1993
Summary: T-bone, the dinosaur, is basically happy, but she thinks of ways to change those around her to make life perfect.

Keller, Beverly. *Pimm's Place*. Coward, McCann & Geoghegan. New York. 1978.
Summary: A timorous young boy teaches his rowdy cousins the value of being quiet and using one's imagination.

Wood, Audrey. *The Napping House*. Harcourt Brace & Co. San Diego. 1984
Summary: In this cumulative tale, a wakeful flea atop a number of sleeping creatures causes a commotion.

Building **Character** Schoolwide

Creating a
Caring Community
in Your School

Take-Home Sheets

Citizenship

"The state of being a citizen with its rights, duties, and privileges."

Suggested Activities:

- Talk to your child about being a good citizen.
- Encourage your child to show good citizenship at school.
- Encourage your child to obey the laws."
- Take your child with you when you vote.
- How can you and your child model good citizenship?

Thought to Ponder:

"One has the right to be wrong in a democracy."

Claude Pepper

Suggested Reading:

The Ox-Cart Man by Donald Hall
Shows daily life in the changing seasons of early 19th century New England.

The Long Way to a New Land by Joan Sandin
Carl Erik journeys with his Family from Sweden to America during the famine of 1868.

Clipper Ship by Thomas P. Lewis
Captain Murdock is accompanied by his family From New York to San Francisco.

Cleanliness

" Clean, Free from dirt; neat and tidy"

Suggested Activities:

- Remind your child to wash his/her hands before eating and after using the restroom.
- Take a bath everyday.
- Brush your teeth daily. (morning, noon, and at bedtime)
- Keep your room neat and clean.
- What other rules of cleanliness do you follow?

Thought to Ponder:

"A clean glove often hides a dirty hand."

English Proverb

Suggested Reading:

No More Baths by Brock Cole
Jessie's family tries to make her take a bath in the middle of the day and she decides to leave home.

Stop Stop by Eddith Thacher Hurd
Miss Muggs almost ruins Suzie's day when she chooses to scrub and clean everyone and everything in sight, until she got drenched herself.

Tidy Titch by Pat Hutchins
Titch helps his older brother and sister clean their rooms.

Confidence

"Bold; courageous, mastering fear"

Suggested Activities:

Make every effort to point out, give examples, and discuss:

- Telling the truth in spite of the consequences.
- Admitting mistakes to others.
- Showing courage in the time of danger.
- Doing the right thing instead of doing what "everyone else" is doing.
- Why is it important to help others in time of need?

Thought to Ponder:

"They conquer who believe they can."

Latin Proverb

Suggested Reading:

Amanda's Poor Self-Image by Geraldine M. Shaheed
An enchanting story of Confidence for all ages.

Alison Rides the Rapids by Nina Alexander
Alison is always up for a good Adventure, but is not sure she wants to be a Junior River Guide.

Jess Was the Brave One by Jean Little
Jess was younger, but she was Braver than her sister Claire, Until one day Claire proved how brave she really was.

Consideration

"To show thoughtfulness or concern for others."

Suggested Activities:

- Talk about ways family members can be considerate of one another.
- Share ways to be be thoughtful of others.
- Do something thoughtful for the teacher.
- Do a thoughtful deed for a neighbor or friend.
- Why should you be considerate of others feelings?

Thought to Ponder:

"The way in which something is given is worth more than the gift itself."

French Proverb

Suggested Reading:

Simple Courtesies by Janet Gallant
The handling of every aspect of our lives effectively.

My Cat Maisie by Pamela Allen
Andrew plays too roughly with a stray cat who comes to his house and the cat runs away.

Consideration by Lucia Raatma
This is a Character Education Book on consideration.

Cooperation

"Working together for a common purpose; joint action."

Suggested Activities:

- Discuss ways to cooperate to get homework done.
- Work cooperatively to prepare dinner.
- Talk about ways to be cooperative at school.
- Discuss how your family can cooperate to get the house chores done.
- Was your family cooperative this week?

Thought to Ponder:

"A sure way for one to lift himself up is by helping to lift someone else."

Booker T. Washington

Suggested Reading:

Not Like That, Like This! by Tony Bradman and Joanna Burroughs
Dad and Thomas go for a walk. They start to tease about how to stick their heads through the iron railing of a fence. Everyone has to cooperate to get Dad unstuck.

Cooperation, Values to Live By by Janet Riehecky
Shows why cooperation is so important.

Courtesy

"Politeness and consideration for others; manners."

Suggested Activities:

Discuss with your child:
- The importance of using good manners.
- The need for considering others' feelings today.
- Wether their friends are courteous or rude to other.
- One rule of courtesy today.
- How were you courteous this week?

Thought to Ponder:

"Each human is uniquely different. Like snowflakes, the human pattern is never cast twice."

Alice Childress

Suggested Reading:

Manners by Aliki
Teaches children about appropriate behavior.

The Please and Thank You Book by Richard Scary
The residents of Busytown Learn useful lessons about manners.

Uncommon Courtesy for Kids by Gregg Harris, Josh Harris, Joshua Harris
Learn 56 ways to be considerate of others in 11 different contexts.

Courage

"To meet a challenge without giving in to fear."

Suggested Activities:

Parents discuss with your child:
- The definition of courage.
- Making an unpopular choice. (e. g. smoking, drinking).
- Being a friend to a new or unpopular student.
- Visiting the dentist, doctor etc.
- Why does it take courage to "do the right thing?"

Thought to Ponder:

"Courage is the first of human qualities because it is the quality which guarantees all others."

Sir Winston Churchill

Suggested Reading:

Emily Just In Time by Jan Slapian & GloCoalson
Emily can now do all kinds of things she could not do when she was younger.

My Brother John by Kristine Church
A younger sister describes her almost fearless older brother.

Anna Banana and Me by Lenore Blegvad
Anna Banana's fearlessness inspires a playmate to face his own fears.

Dependability

"To depend on, rely upon, to trust."

Suggested Activities:

- Have your child to assist you in doing a dependable task.
- Teach your child the necessity for taking important telephone messages.
- Give your child the responsibility for feeding the family pet.
- Allow your child to fix a family snack or meal.
- Why it is important to be dependable?

Thought to Ponder:

"You cannot escape the responsibility of tomorrow by evading it today."

Abraham Lincoln

Suggested Reading:

Mystery of the Lost Letter by Olive Blake
Jane is sent to the post office to mail a very important letter, but realizes it is missing after buying a stamp.

Mike Mulligan and His Steam Shovel by Virginia Lee Burton
Mike proves that his steam shovel is dependable even though it is old.

Responsibility:What Is It? by J. Riehecky & N. Pemberton
This book suggest ways to be responsible.

Fairness

"Equitable; according to the rules; honest; just."

Suggested Activities:

- Share ideas about fairness with the family.
- Remind your child to play fairly.
- Discuss the day's events in terms of fairness.
- Discuss how to handle an unfair situation.
- How are you fair to others?

Thought to Ponder:

"What we see depends mainly on what we look for."

John Lubbock

Suggested Reading:

The Cow of No Color by Nina Jaffe, Steve Zenith, & Whitney Sherman
A collection of stories from around the world where the characters face problem situations requiring decisions about what is fair or just.

No Fair! by Caren Holtzman
A story about fairness when Kristy and David cannot agree.

It's Not Fair! by Dominique Jolin
A young girl complains to her father about what the other children get to do. Her father's reply is a heart warming story.

Generosity

"Willing to give and share, unselfish."

Suggested Activities:

- Discuss being giving to a sibling or another family member.
- Discuss giving unselfishly of yourself to help others.
- Discuss sharing time with your friends.
- Discuss how your child feels when being generous to others.
- Why is it better to give than to receive?

Thought to Ponder:

"I just wanted to make a difference, however small, in the world."

Arthur Ashe

Suggested Reading:

The Giving Tree by Shel Silverstein
This story of a boy who grows to manhood, and of a tree that gives him her bounty through the years, is a moving parable about the gift of giving and the capacity to love.

The Book of Giving by Kay Chorao
A collection of poems from such well known writers as Robert Louis Stevenson, Langston Hughes, and Margaret Wise Brown, as well as lesser known poets from other countries, captures the pleasures of being young.

Goodwill

"Showing kindness and friendliness, giving and sharing"

Suggested Activities:

- Do an act of kindness. (e.g. walk a neighbor's dog, go to the grocery, run an errand for a shut in.)
- Make a get-well card for a sick friend.
- Give items to the Goodwill of Salvation Army.
- Join the Boy/Girl Scouts or 4H Group.
- What goodwill have you shown to others this week?

Thought to Ponder:

"Ask not what your country can do for you—ask what you can do for your Country."

John F. Kennedy

Suggested Reading:

Jonathan and His Mommy by Irene Smalls
As a mother and son explore their neighborhood, they try various ways of walking—from giant steps and reggae steps to criss cross steps and backwards steps.

The Long Winter by Laura Ingalls Wilder
A dangerous trip is made to secure wheat for a starving village, during a terrible winter.

Python's Party by Brian Wildsmith
The animals are wary when hungry Python invites them to a party to show goodwill.

Honesty

"Truthful, fair, trustworthy."

Suggested Activities:

- Discuss why it is important to tell the truth.
- Share feelings about how it feels to blame others for something you did wrong.
- Share your feeling about children that take things that do not belong to them.
- Discuss your views about children who cheat to get good grades.
- Why is "honesty" always the best policy.

Thought to Ponder:

"A half-truth is a whole lie."

Author unknown

Suggested Reading:

Believing Sophie by H.J. Hutchins
An obnoxious lady at the grocery store mistakenly accuses young Sophie of shoplifting, and Sophie must prove her innocence. The storekeeper lets her go, but Sophie isn't sure he believes her.

Arthur in a Pickle by Marc Tolon Brown
Arthur must report to the principal's office first thing tomorrow morning for telling Mr. Ratburn his dog ate his homework.

Independence

"Freedom; Reliance on one's own efforts."

Suggested Activities:

- Discuss the meaning of the word independence with your child.
- Give your child permission to do a task independently.
- Let your child do his/her homework independently.
- Read one of the suggested books about independence to your child.
- How can your child be independent at school?

Thought to Ponder:

"There can be no real freedom without the freedom to fail."

Eric Hoofer

Suggested Reading:

Do Not Open by Briton Turkle
Following a storm Miss Moody and her cat find an intriguing bottle washed up on the beach. Should they ignore its "Do not open" warning?

Wagon Wheels by Barbara Brenner
The pioneer story of one black family's journey westward to a new home.

Initiative

"Ability to get things done without being told."

Suggested Activities:

Talk to your child about doing the following without being told:
- Practicing playing your instrument without being told.
- Doing homework.
- Making the bed.
- Take the initiative to do a task without being asked.
- Have you taken the initiative to recycle paper, cans, or glass etc.?

Thought to Ponder:

"Well begun is half done."

Proverb

Suggested Reading:

Palm Trees, by Nancy Cote
When Millie has to fix her hair by herself for the first time, her friend Renee and a sense of humor help her to discover something about friendship and independence.

The Girl Who Owened a City by O.T. Nelson
When a plague sweeps over the earth killing everyone except children under twelve, ten-year-old Lisa organizes a group to rebuild a new way of life.

A Weed Is A Flower by Aliki
Brief text and pictures present the life of the man, born a slave, who became a scientist and devoted his entire life to helping the South improve its agriculture.

Joyfulness

"A strong feeling of happiness, contentment or satisfaction"

Suggested Activities:

- Discuss something good your child did today. (e.g. Did a good deed for someone else).
- Smile more today.
- Do something to make your child happy.
- Plan a family activity.
- Has anything made you happy this week?

Thought to Ponder:

"Laughter softens life's rough edges."

Cherie Carter-Scott

Suggested Reading:

Life Is Fun **by Nancy Carlson**
Whimsical instructions on how to be happy on earth while providing advice on how to get the most out of life.

The Child's World of Joy **by Jane Belk Moncure**
Simple text and scenes depict such joys as the first snowman of the year, flying a kite, holding a baby sister for the first time, and being hugged by Mom and Dad after they've been away on a trip.

Shine, Sun **by Carol Greene**
A child's happy reaction to the sun.

Kindness

"Willing to help; gentle; friendly; sympathetic."

Suggested Activities:

- Share ideas about how your child can be kind to family members.
- Discuss how your child can be kind to family pet(s).
- Display kindness to your child today.
- Help others.
- What kind deeds have you done this week?

Thought to Ponder:

"The way something is given is worth more than the gift itself."

French Proverb

Suggested Reading:

Kids' Random Acts of Kindness by Dawna Markova (Intro. by Rosalynn Carter)
Inspirational stories of generosity and kindness.

Andy and the Lion by James Daugherty
Andy meets a lion on the way to school and wins his friendship for life by removing a thorn from his paw.

Caring by Shelly Neilsen
Poems about children being thoughtful and kind.

Loyalty

"Faithful, especially to ones country, team, friend, duty or obligations."

Suggested Activities:

- Discuss family loyalty.
- Show loyalty to your friends.
- Discuss ways to show loyalty at school.
- Read a book to your child from the suggested reading list.
- Is it easy to be loyal on a consistent basis?

Thought to Ponder:

"When you're loyal to someone or something, you're faithful, constant, and dependable."

Anonymous

Suggested Reading:

Best Friends by Steven Kellogg
The twins' close friendship is threatened when Jessica is admitted to an exclusive girls' club.

Four Good Friends by Jock Curle
Maria, the woodcutter's wife, befriends four hungry animals who teach her husband the value of loyal friendship when he goes to jail.

A Friend for Caitlin by Lynea Bowdish & Meredith Johnson
Caitlin's best friend moved away. Caitlin discovers that sometimes our dearest friends are right under our noses.

Neatness

Orderly, tidy, and clean

Suggested Activities:

- Ask your child to write his/her spelling words in alphabetical order.
- Ask your child to keep his/her room neat and clean.
- Explain to your child why there has to be order in a courtroom.
- Explain to your children why they should put their toys away after playing.
- Why is the dictionary written in alphabetical order?

Thought to Ponder:

"If each one sweeps before his own door, the whole street will be clean."

Yiddish Proverb

Suggested Reading:

Tidy Titch by Pat Hutchins
Basking in the satisfaction of his own clean room, young. Titch offers to help out his older, less tidy siblings, but when their rooms reveal a treasury of old toys, Titch's room loses its own spotless state

The Twins by John Wallace
Lil and Nelly are twins. Lil is neat and tidy. Nelly is very messy. Lil likes pink things and sensible shoes. Nelly likes oil and fast food. The twins are always fighting but together they make the perfect team.

Patience

"The ability to wait calmly; tolerance."

Suggested Activities:

- Talk to your child/children about being tolerant of younger siblings.
- Teach your child to raise his/her hand and wait to be recognized by the teacher while in class.
- Model patience while playing a game.
- Demonstrate patience while waiting in line. (e.g. at the bus stop, at a concert etc.)
- Discuss ways you/your child have modeled patience this week.

Thought to Ponder:

"One thing today, another tomorrow."

Spanish Proverb

Suggested Reading:

Bear's Christmas Surprise by Elizabeth Winthrop
A talking stuffed bear is remorseful after he peeks at his Christmas packages while playing hide-and-seek with his baby sitter, but Nora, his owner, forgives him, and a happy holiday ensues.

Not Yet, Yvette by Helen Ketteman
All through the day, Yvette asks, "Is it time yet, Dad?" Dad answers, "Not yet, Yvette". Then Yvette and her dad get busy because there's a lot to do before Mom's surprise birthday party.

Patriotism

"Love, respect and loyalty to one's country."

Suggested Activities:

- Recite the Pledge of Allegiance.
- Look up information about the Liberty Bell.
- Visit the Statue of Liberty.
- Fly the American flag at your house.
- Discuss these American symbols and their importance.
- How many other symbols can you name?

Thought to Ponder:

"I only regret that I have but one life to lose for my country."

Nathan Hale

Suggested Reading:

I Pledge Allegiance by June Swanson
Describes how and why the Pledge of Allegiance was written, how it has changed in wording over the years, and precisely what it means.

Celebrations by Myra C. Livingston
A collection of poems on the holidays of the year.

Day by Day Activity Book by Susan Ohanian
365 Days of fun ideas for parents, teachers & kids.

Peacefulness

"The state of being calm, tranquil and quiet."

Suggested Activities:

- Discuss peaceful ways to resolve conflict.
- Share a quiet evening meal with your family.
- After a stressful situation help your child to remain calm.
- Be calm during a crisis. (e.g. a fire, tornado, or an accident)
- Are you a peaceful person?

Thought to Ponder:

" Much happiness is overlooked because it doesn't cost anything."

Author Unknown

Suggested Reading:

What Do You Stand For? by Barbara A. Lewis
True stories profile kids who exemplify positive traits and in- spiring quotations set the stage for kids to think about, discuss and debate positive traits.

Heartprints by P.K. Hallinan
The ways readers can leave heartprints wherever they go.

The Napping House by Audrey Wood
In this cumulative tale, a wakeful flea atop a number of sleeping creatures causes a commotion, with just one bite.

Perseverance

"Steadily working in spite of difficulties, without giving up."

Suggested Activities:

- Discuss going to school in inclement weather.
- Share three ways to help your child to accomplish a difficult task.
- Remind your child to practice reading daily.
- Be persistent in helping your child with their problem subject area.
- Why should you put more effort into accomplishing a difficult task?

Thought to Ponder:

"Learning is not attained by chance, it must be sought for with ardor and attended to with diligence."

Abigail Adams

Suggested Reading:

The Waiting Day by Harriet Diller
A beggar teaches a busy ferryman an important lesson about the right way to use time.

Max's Breakfast by Rosemary Wells
Max's sister tries hardto get him to eat his breakfast egg.

Barbie: Practice Makes Perfect by Mona Miller
Everyone in Barbie's class does well but one. A girl named Diane falls again and again and is too discouraged to continue. After a few weeks of special coaching by Barbie, Diane dares to return to the boardwalk.

Politeness

"Showing consideration for others, refined, cultured, mannerly"

Suggested Activities:

Parents, try this quiz with your child:
- If you need to interrupt an adult. You should say _____.
- Mom thanks you for taking out the trash. You say_____.
- You receive a compliment from someone. You say_____.
- You want to go to a friend's house. You say _____.
- When Mom/Dad buy you something. You should say_____.

Thought to Ponder:

"We cannot always oblige, but we can always speak obligingly."

Voltaire

Suggested Reading:

Mary Louise Loses Her Manners by Diane Cuneo
Mary Louise shocks her family by making rude comments.

What Do You Say Dear by Sesyle Joslin
Advice on how to cope correctly with a variety of situations.

Bad Habits by Babette Cole
Lueretzia Crum's nicer bad habits are appealing to her classmates and they want to be like her.

Promptness

"Ready, quick, being on time."

Suggested Activities:

- Explain why it is important to do things on time.
- Give your child a set amount of time to complete a task.
- Make sure your child is on time for school today.
- Discuss why it is important to respect other's time.
- Why do you have to be on time for a flight?

Thought to Ponder:

"The time is always right to do what is right."

Martin Luther King Jr.

Suggested Reading:

The Boy Who Was Always Late by John Patrick Norman McHennessy
A teacher regrets his decision to disbelieve a student's outlandish excuses for being tardy.

The Easter Bunny That Overslept by Priscilla Fredrich
Having slept past Easter, the Easter bunny tries to distribute his eggs on Mother's Day, the Fourth of July, and Halloween, but no one is interested. At Christmas time it is Santa who gets him back on track.

Punctuality

"Being on time, prompt, acting at the right time"

Suggested Activities:

- Share with your child the importance of being on time for school, work, dinner, etc.
- Discuss consequences of being late.
- Have your child plan an activity for the weekend involving being punctual.
- Plan scheduled "family time" every week.
- Were there problems caused by not being on time this week?

Thought to Ponder:

"The early bird gets the worm."

Old Proverb

Suggested Reading:

It's About time by Nancy White Carlstrom
From early morning to bedtime, rhymes present the activities of Jesse Bear as he dresses, plays, eats, and gets ready for bed.

Around the Clock With Harriet by Betsy & Guilio Maestro
A book about telling time.

The Berenstain Bears Catch The Bus by Stan & Jan Berenstain
As the minutes pass and the school bus gets closer to their house, Brother and Sister aren't even up yet.

Readiness

"Prepared for immediate action; prepared, mentally fit"

Suggested Activities:

- Help your child to be prepare for school by getting plenty of rest and eating right.
- Insure your child has completed his/her home work and is prepared for school.
- Help your child study for a test.
- Say something positive to your child to help start the day on a positive note.
- Have your child select what they would like to wear the next day.

Thought to Ponder:

"The great secret of success in life is to be ready when opportunity comes."

Benjamin Disraeli

Suggested Reading:

Be Ready at Eight by Peggy Parish
All day long, Miss Molly keeps meeting people reminding her to "be ready at eight," but Miss Molly cannot think why they are telling her this.

The House with a Clock in Its Walls by John Bellairs
A boy goes to live with his magician uncle in a mansion that has a clock hidden in the walls.

Resourcefulness

**"Skillful and imaginative in finding ways
of doing things or resolving difficulties."**

Suggested Activities:

- Talk to your child about saving a part of his allowance every week.
- Teach your child the importance of recycling.
- Teach your child how to shop resourcefully.
- Read a suggested book about being resourceful to your child.
- Were you able to be thrifty this week?

Thought to Ponder:

"To turn an obstacle to ones advantage is a great step towards victory".

French Proverb

Suggested Reading:

Joseph Had A Little Overcoat by Simms Taback
learn that you can always make something, even out of nothing.

Lost in the Woods by Colleen Politano
what a well-informed, resourceful child should do when faced with a frightening situation.

Respectfulness

"To have or show high regard for; esteem, honor."

Suggested Activities:

- Have a family talk about respect after reading one of the suggested books with your children.
- Respect your child's opinion.
- Teach your child to respect their neighbor's property and privacy. (i.e. playing loud music, playing on neighbor's lawn, picking their flowers, etc.)
- Teach your child proper respect for others. (Say Please; Thank-you; You are welcome, etc.)
- Do other people respect you?

Thought to Ponder:

"We must learn to live together as brothers or perish together as fools."

Martin Luther King Jr.

Suggested Reading:

Respect by Beverly Fiday & Deborah Crowdy
Shows ways children show respect.

Respect (Learn the Value of Series) by Elaine P. Goley
Defines the concept of respect by examples of how it may be shown in daily life.

Responsibility

"To be able to carry out a duty; trustworthy; reliable."

Suggested Activities:

- Discuss with your child ways he/she can be more responsible at home.
- Talk to your child about being a responsible safety patrol person.
- Assign special daily/weekly tasks to your child or children.
- Teach your child that he/she is responsible for his/her own actions. (e.g. not talking to strangers, not smoking or drinking, or not taking drugs.)
- Did you act responsibly this week?

Thought to Ponder:

"You cannot escape the responsibility of tomorrow by evading it today."

Abraham Lincoln

Suggested Reading:

Arthur's Computer Disaster by Elaine P. Goley
Arthur knows he's not supposed to be using his mother's computer, but the lure of "Deep,Dark Sea," the greatest game in the universe, is irresistible.

A Child's Book of Responsibilities by Marjorie R. Nelsen
This book teaches your child To be responsible and enjoy choosing task to do.

Self-Control

"Control of ones emotions or actions."

Activities for Parents:

- Identify an area of behavior your child needs to work on to help control actions/emotions such as anger, fear, etc.
- Practice controlling your anger.
- List ways to help you continue to control your behavior.
- Think before you act.
- Were you able to change your or your child's behavior in a positive way this week?

Thought to Ponder:

"If it is not right, do not do it; if it is not true, do not say it."

Marcus Aurelius

Suggested Reading:

When Sophie Gets Angry by Molly Garrett Bang
The rage a girl experiences when her sister takes her toy away.

The Biggest Pest on Eighth Avenue by Laurie Lawlor
Mary Lou and her friends are working to perform a play of their own creation, but their planning sessions are continually interrupted by Mary Lou's pesky brother, Tommy.

Self-Discipline

"To control of one's actions or emotions."

Suggested Activities:

- Discuss the consequences of telling a lie.
- Practice being a good sport.
- List ways to be self-disciplined even when you are angry.
- Think before you act. (e.g. Letting others talk you into fighting)
- Can you practice self-discipline daily?

Thought to Ponder:

"It is easier to talk than hold one's tongue."

Greek Proverb

Suggested Reading:

All Alone After School by Muriel Stanek
When his mother must take a job and can't afford a babysitter, a young boy gradually develops confidence about staying home alone after school.

I Was So Mad by Mercer Mayer
A child tries a variety of ways to dissolve anger.

Don't Laugh Joe by Keiko Kasza
While practicing playing dead, Little Joe Possum always gets the giggles.

Self-Reliance

"Relying on one's own abilities, efforts or judgement."

Suggested Activities:

- Assign your child a chore for which he/she is solely responsible. (e.g. Caring for the family pet.)
- Monitor your child keeping his/her room clean.
- Monitor your child fixing his/her lunch for school tomorrow.
- Assign your child the responsibility of doing a homework assignment independently.
- Discuss with your child how he/she demonstrated self-reliance during the week.

Thought to Ponder:

"You have to expect things of yourself before you can do them."

Michael Jordan

Suggested Reading:

***Arthur's Pet Business* by Marc Brown**
Arthur's determination to prove he is responsible enough to have a puppy.

***The Hating Book* by Charlotte Zolotow**
A little girl has an argument with her friend. She uses self-control to apologize.

***I Can Do That* by Sally Schaedler**
A book about confidence.

Sportsmanship

Using fair play or sportsmanlike conduct.

Suggested Activities:

Parents discuss with your child:
- What it means to be a "good sport."
- Losing a very import game.
- The joys of winning.
- The importance of being a team player.
- Why should you have good conduct when playing a sport?

Thought to Ponder:

"A cheerful loser is a winner."

Elbert Hubbard

Suggested Reading:

Abby the Bad Sport by Ann Matthews Martin
Abby loves soccer and joins the team thinking she'll be the star, but Erin just might be better.

Let's Talk About Being a Bad Sport by Joy Wilt Berry
Behavior of both a bad and a good sport.

Keep Your Old Hat by Anna Grossnickle Hines
Young children learn the necessity of compromise.

Obedience

"The act, habit, or condition of obeying; compliance with rules, regulations, or laws.

Suggested Activities:

Discuss with your child:
- What it means to be obedient.
- Obeying school rules, classroom rules, cafeteria and bus rules.
- Knowing the difference between right and wrong.
- Respecting our laws.
- Why should children be obedient?

Thought to Ponder:

"No man is above the law and no man is below it; nor do we ask any man's permission when we require him to obey it."

Theodore Roosevelt

Suggested Reading:

It's a Spoon, Not a Shovel by Caralyn Buehner
A handsome combination of humor, puzzles, and lessons in elementary good behavior.

4B Goes Wild by Jamie Gilson
Fourth graders on a three-day camping trip with their teachers experience frights and delights.

I Did It, I'm Sorry by Caralyn Buehner
This hilarious quiz book points the way to good behavior, presenting a series of animals facing moral dilemmas.

Thankfulness

"To feel or express gratitude; grateful."

Suggested Activities:

Ask your child to show thankfulness by:
- Remembering to say please and thank you.
- Giving a few words of thanks before eating.
- Sharing a picture of something you are thankful for at school or home.
- Helping someone less fortunate. (Give several items to the charity.)
- Has your child done a good deed for the teacher this week?

Thought to Ponder:

"There is as much greatness of mind in acknowledging a good turn, as in doing it.

Senecca

Suggested Reading:

Casey the Greedy Young Cowboy by Michael P. Waite
A book about being thankful.

Thankfulness by Janet McDonnell
Describes thankful feelings.

I never Say I'm Thankful, But I Am by Jane Belk Moncure
A child thinks aloud about all the things for which he is grateful.

Tolerance

"Acceptance of individual differences."

Suggested Activities:

- Discuss attitudes and biases toward people.
- Show tolerance for others.
- Discuss with your child being tolerant of handicapped people.
- Ask your child to share feelings with you about being tolerant during a difficult situation.
- Why should one be tolerant of others?

Thought to Ponder:

"With compassion, we see benevolently our own human condition and the condition of our fellow beings. We drop prejudice. We withhold judgment."

Christina Baldwin

Suggested Reading:

Claudia's Big Party by Ann Matthews Martin
Claudia's loving the October weather and her many friends, both in school and in the BSC. But when she throws a party to bring her two groups of pals together, she creates more problems than she solves.

Talking Walls by Mary Burns Knight
Attempts to dissolve cultural barriers and emphasize a sense of place by depicting different host children telling the histories of the walls in their communities. All ages.

Truthfulness

"Telling the truth; being true, honest, and sincere."

Suggested Activities:

Parents, model truthfulness by:

Answering a telephone call instead of saying you are not home.

Stopping at a stop sign instead of just pausing.

Giving back money if you are given too much change.

Being honest about breaking something.

Did you model truthfulness all week?

Thought to Ponder:

"Truth is always the strongest argument."

Sophocles

Suggested Reading:

Franklin Fibs by Paulette Bourgeois
Franklin a tells fib and is asked to prove it

On My Honor by Marion Dane Bauer
When his best friend drowns while they are swimming in a treacherous river that they had promised never to go near, Joel is devastated and terrified at having to tell both sets of parents the terrible consequences of their disobedience.

Uniqueness

"One of a kind."

Suggested Activities:

- Discuss being an individual.
- Give your child permission to help a neighbor or relative to do a special task.
- Take your child to the library and help pick out a book about a unique individual.
- Let you child do a unique task. (e.g. Make a new desert for dinner.)
- How can you be unique as a parent?

Thought to Ponder:

"Each human is uniquely different. Like snowflakes, the human pattern is never cast twice."

Alice Childress

Suggested Reading:

Ugly Duckling by Jerry Pinkney
Andersen's story of the duckling who became a swan.

Just a Little Different by Mercer Mayer
A new kid who is just a little different moves in next door to Little Critter and his family.